Exploring C.H. Spurgeon's key to ministerial success

"If you love the life and legacy of Charles Spurgeon, or you want to know what spiritual giants contributed to his deep spirituality, or you are serious about serving God, or you want to be infectious with your passion for the gospel, you need to read this book. Bob Penhearow digs into the best and serves up a book that will motivate you to holy lifestyle and Christ-honouring service."

—DR. STEPHEN BECK

Professor of Practical Theology, Freie Theologische Hochschule Giessen, Germany; European Director of City Mentoring Program; pastor, church planter and author of *Smartbuilder: A God-centred spirituality in a Me-centred world*

"This is not simply another volume on 'The Prince of Preachers' or a new 'how-to' manual for successful ministry by today's standards. Bob Penhearow writes glowingly about C.H. Spurgeon's spirituality as the wellspring of his powerful and fruitful ministry. A refreshing call to true pastoral ministry marked by deep love for Christ, personal holiness, and unshakeable confidence in the gospel. Read it and be encouraged."

—DR. RAYMOND MARTIN

Pastor of Trinity Baptist Church, Allentown, Pennsylvania, USA, and teacher for Carey Outreach Ministries in the Far East

---

"This book by Bob Penhearow helpfully explores this vital connection between piety and ministerial success in both Spurgeon's life and also in that of the three most prominent Baptist leaders before Spurgeon who shaped his thinking: John Bunyan, John Gill and Andrew Fuller. He helps us understand how these men defined true success and the way they connected it to spirituality. This is much-needed study and I, for one, am very glad it has been published."

—from the FOREWORD by DR. MICHAEL A.G. HAYKIN

Professor of Church History and Biblical Spirituality at Southern Baptist Theological Seminary, Louisville, Kentucky, USA, and director of The Andrew Fuller Center for Baptist Studies

It will be in vain for me to stock my library, or organize societies, or project schemes, if I neglect the culture of myself; for books, and agencies, and systems, are only remotely the instruments of my holy calling; my own spirit, soul, and body, are my nearest machinery for sacred service; my spiritual faculties, and my inner life, are my battle ax and weapons of war.

Lord sanctify us. Oh! that Thy Spirit would come and saturate every faculty, subdue every passion, and use every power of our nature for obedience to God. Come, Holy Spirit, we do know Thee; Thou hast often overshadowed us. Come, more fully take possession of us.

—Charles Haddon Spurgeon

Charles Haddon Spurgeon
(1834–1892)

EXPLORING
C.H. SPURGEON'S
KEY TO MINISTERIAL SUCCESS

Bob Penhearow

CAREY
PRINTING PRESS

CAREY
PRINTING PRESS

Published by
Carey Outreach Ministries Inc., Guelph, Ontario, Canada
www.careyoutreach.org

About us
Carey Printing Press is the publishing arm of Carey Outreach Ministries, an international Christian organization that provides theological training to spiritual leaders to shape the church and influence the nations.
General editor: Bob Penhearow

First published 2011

Cover and book design by Janice Van Eck

Library and Archives Canada Cataloguing in Publication

Penhearow, Bob
    Exploring C.H. Spurgeon's key to ministerial success / Bob Penhearow.

Includes bibliographical references and index.
ISBN 978-0-9876841-0-3

    1. Spurgeon, C. H. (Charles Haddon), 1834–1892. 2. Bunyan, John, 1628–1688—Influence. 3. Gill, John, 1697–1771—Influence. 4. Fuller, Andrew, 1754–1815—Influence. 5. Baptists—England—Clergy—Biography. 6. Spirituality. I. Title.

BX6495.S7P45 2011   286'.1092   C2011-904890-6

To Dorothy, my darling wife,
God's precious gift to me
and to this ministry

.

Contents

Foreword

In many ways, C.H. Spurgeon's ministry was nothing less than amazing: the crowded auditories that assembled to hear the "Cambridgeshire lad" in the 1850s and that continued unabated till the end of his ministry in the early 1890s; the remarkable conversions that occurred under his preaching and the numerous churches in metropolitan London and the county of Surrey that owed their origins to his evangelical activism; the solid Puritan divinity that undergirded his evangelical convictions—something of a rarity in the heyday of the Victorian era during which he ministered for that was a day imbued with the very different ambience of Romanticism; and finally, the ongoing life of his sermons that are still being widely read around the world today and deeply appreciated by God's children.

What accounts for all of this? Numerous reasons could be cited, many of which may indeed play a secondary role in his ministerial success. For example, Mike Nicholls emphasizes the importance of Spurgeon's voice to his success as a preacher. He possessed, Nicholls writes, "one of the great speaking voices of his age, musical and combining compass, flexibility and power."[1] Augustine Birrell (1850–1933), the son of one of Spurgeon's fellow Baptist pastors and who served as

---

1 Mike Nicholls, *C.H. Spurgeon: The Pastor Evangelist* (Didcot: Baptist Historical Society, 1992), 37.

the Chief Secretary for Ireland from 1907 to 1916, testifies to this fact. Birrell records that once when he went to hear Spurgeon preach, the only seat he could find was in the topmost gallery, in what the English call "the gods." He was squished between a woman eating an orange and a man sucking peppermints. Finding this combination of odours unendurable, he was about to leave, when, he said, "I heard a voice and forgot all else."[2] But Spurgeon himself looked to quite a different source for the blessings that attended his ministry. In a speech that he gave at a celebration held in honour of his fiftieth birthday in 1884, the Baptist preacher forthrightly declared that the blessing he had enjoyed in his pastorate "must be entirely attributed to the grace of God, and to the working of God's Holy Spirit.... Let that stand as a matter, not only taken for granted, but as a fact distinctly recognized."[3] In other words: behind Spurgeon's successes as a minister of the gospel was his walk with God.

Today we tend to separate success and spirituality. For those of us who delight in "the Puritanic writers," as Spurgeon once called them,[4] we usually emphasize piety but are wary of being successful. On the other hand, those who write books and give talks on being successful in one's Christian ministry and how to grow your church seem to give nary a thought to piety as part of the package of success. Spurgeon, though, is concerned about both. This book by Bob Penhearow helpfully explores this vital connection between piety and ministerial success in both Spurgeon's life and also in that of the three most prominent Baptist leaders before Spurgeon who shaped his thinking: John Bunyan, John Gill and Andrew Fuller. He helps us understand how these men defined true success and the way they connected it to spirituality. This is much-needed study and I, for one, am very glad it has been published.

Michael A.G. Haykin

---

2   Cited E.J. Poole-Connor, *Evangelicalism in England* (London: The Fellowship of Independent Evangelical Churches, 1951), 226–227.

3   *C.H. Spurgeon's Autobiography*, compiled Susannah Spurgeon and J.W. Harrald (London: Passmore and Alabaster, 1900), IV, 243.

4   *The Metropolitan Tabernacle Pulpit*, 9:668.

Acknowledgements

This book would not have been completed without Dr. Michael Haykin's abounding patience, insightful knowledge, eagle eyes, rock-sure guiding hand, sharp pen and encouraging heart. Dr. Haykin's enthusiasm and graciousness has made this project a delight, a learning experience and a personal blessing.

Gratitude is also expressed to our readers: Janet Billson and Pastor Joseph Gray for their diligent perusal of the manuscript, and helpful suggestions.

A special thanks goes to Linda Billson for her patient endurance in helping prepare the manuscript for publication.

Heartfelt recognition is also expressed to Janice Van Eck for her meticulousness and organizational skills in editing and preparing this manuscript and book cover for final publication. Thank you, Janice!

Also, I would like to acknowledge my dear wife Dorothy, a precious gift from God and my partner in life and ministry. Without her firmness in "cracking the whip," loving support and unwavering confidence in her husband, this project would not have seen the light of day.

Introduction

This book advocates that spirituality is an essential prerequisite to ministerial blessing. This was indeed the lifelong conviction of C.H. Spurgeon, as well as other well-known and influential Baptist giants. In this regard, C.H. Spurgeon's personal piety is presented as a model for ministerial success for the twenty-first-century pastor.

Yet we must ask, what is ministerial success? What is piety? What is spirituality? Both ministerial success and spirituality are interpreted very differently throughout Christendom, which inevitably leads to confusion, coloured by one's own presuppositions. Ministerial success and spirituality need defining, at least how Spurgeon and other notable Baptists have understood them.

Many think that to be a successful minister you must serve large crowds each Sunday, or perhaps possess copious amounts of pulpit eloquence, or fame. Yet this is not how ministerial success is understood biblically. It is not found in numbers, though they are wonderful to behold; it is not in the minister's eloquence, yet it is desirous to speak well; nor is it found in fame or the magnitude of the church's budget, although it is wonderful for a church or ministry not to be strapped for funds. No, ministerial success is found in being captive to the Word of God. It is found in being faithful to the gospel that God has transmitted and entrusted to his people. Spurgeon knew well that

xviii *Exploring C.H. Spurgeon's key to ministerial success*

God's Word never returns void, and the minister who upholds and fleshes out God's Word—even if he plods on facing apparent failure—will find himself successful. Success, then, is found in faithfulness to God, expressed in a rock-sure stand on God's eternal Word—*sola Scriptura*.

Spirituality is another vague term. Many think of spirituality as nebulous, a spiritual person being someone who is "out there." We think of spiritual people as being those who spend their time thinking great theological thoughts that are too deep and profound for the average person to comprehend. This is an unfortunate misrepresentation of spirituality. A spiritual man, as we will see with Spurgeon, is one who is in step with God's Spirit, empowered by his Spirit. A spiritual man is one who walks in close communion with God through prayer and supplication. A spiritual man is one whose heart delights in God and burns for the glory of his God. A spiritual man seeks to obey the Word of God. He talks the talk and walks the walk, seeking to apply the gospel message to his listeners and to himself. He is sincere, honest and fruitful in his endeavours for the Lord. His theology is an applied theology; his theology is a springboard to doxology. He lives for God, God's glory alone—*soli Deo Gloria*.

Having defined the terms, the book sets the scene with a brief sketch of Spurgeon's life followed by a look at the lives of a number of Calvinistic Baptist giants—John Bunyan, John Gill and Andrew Fuller—all of whom tenaciously advocated spirituality as an essential prerequisite for ministerial blessing and whose writings greatly influenced the mind, heart and ministry of C.H. Spurgeon.

Spurgeon's convictions about the power of holiness and godliness in the lives of ministers to impact their ministries are then examined through his lectures and sermons to ministerial students at his Pastors' College. This is followed by a practical look at Spurgeon's personal spirituality as evidenced in his hymn-writing, prayers, family life, worship, personal relationships, letter-writing, sermons and general lifestyle.

Having established that spirituality is essential for ministerial success, the book seeks to promote spirituality via a practical workbook (see "Appendix"), to encourage personal piety for today's pastors and spiritual leaders.

My prayer is that the Lord would be pleased to raise up spiritual leaders whose hearts truly burn for the glory of God, delighting in the beauty and wonder of Christ—who alone is the sovereign King of kings and Lord of every lord.

C.H. Spurgeon

1

Overview of the life and ministry of C.H. Spurgeon

The social and political scene

Victorian England spread her mighty wings across the globe. The British Empire's vast conquests, combined with various colonization programmes, ensured that England was at the centre of the known world. Wealth and power flowed from the four corners of the British Empire to the shores of England, and specifically to the upper classes and aristocracy.

Sadly, oppression and exploitation of the working class continued. Often the working classes were uneducated and rejected. Moral decay was evidenced everywhere. Prostitution flourished in the cities, young girls leaving their homes and villages behind to survive by selling their bodies. Gin houses flourished where the pain produced by the toil and suffering of daily existence was dulled. Workhouses sprang up to exploit the orphans and the disadvantaged; these were the dark and difficult days of "Oliver Twist."[1]

---

1 Oliver Twist is the protagonist of the novel *Oliver Twist* (1838) by Charles Dickens. For detailed analysis and statistics regarding the appalling social conditions of Victorian London in 1869, consult James Greenwood. Greenwood listed seven curses in London

The spiritual scene

Although England had benefited greatly from the revivals of George Whitefield (1714–1770) and John Wesley (1703–1791), the pulpits of the land were largely replaced with eloquence and rhetoric at the cost of a life-giving and life-transforming gospel. The clergy were seen as professionals rather than receiving their high and holy calling from God. Modernism and Liberalism would soon sweep across the land in the 1860s to impact the church in the 1880s. Evolution would further make its inroads, shake, and shatter the faith of many. Certain coldness, even callousness, existed towards God's Word. Spurgeon graphically describes the spiritual condition of England during his ministry:

> We live in perilous times; we are passing through a most eventful period; the Christian world is convulsed; there is a mighty upheaval of the old foundations of faith; a great over-hauling of old teaching. The Bible is made to speak today in an unknown tongue. Gospel teachings, the proclamation of which made men fear to sin and dread the thought of eternity, are being shelved. Calvary is being robbed of its glory, sin of its horror, and the power of the gospel weakened. There is no use in mincing matters; there are thousands of us in all denominations who believe that many ministers have seriously departed from the truths of the gospel, and a sad decline of spiritual life is manifest in our churches.... The case is mournful. Certain ministers are making infidels. Avowed atheists are not a tenth as dangerous as those preachers who scatter doubt and stab at faith. A plain man told us the other day that two ministers had derided him, because he thought we should pray for rain.... Have these advanced thinkers filled their own chapels? Have they, after all, prospered through discarding the old methods? The places which the old Gospel filled, the new nonsense has emptied and will keep empty.[2]

---

in his day as: neglected children, professional thieves, professional beggars, fallen women, the curse of drunkenness, betting gamblers and the waste of charity [*The Seven Curses of London* (www.victorianlondon.org, 1869), accessed February 6, 2003].

2   James T. Allen, *Life Story of C.H. Spurgeon* (1893; reprint, Albany: Ages Software, 1996), 30–31.

In the midst of this spiritual darkness and moral decay, God sovereignly raised up a number of champions who stood firm for the faith, whose pulpits boldly declared the gospel. For example, Bishop J.C. Ryle of Liverpool (1816–1900), Alexander McLaren of Manchester (1832–1907), F.B. Meyer, (1847–1929), Joseph Parker (1830–1902) and William Booth (1829–1912), founder of the Salvation Army, to name but a few. Yet the greatest of them all, the one hailed as the best of the best, "The Prince of Preachers," was Charles Haddon Spurgeon (1834–1892). Spurgeon would thunder forth the gospel for over forty years from the pulpit of the Metropolitan Tabernacle, situated at Elephant and Castle, South London. His gospel zeal through numerous ministries would shake the English nation and reverberate around the world.

Early years

Spurgeon was born on June 19, 1834, in the quaint village of Kelvedon, Essex. He came from steadfast Puritan stock with historic traditions of nonconformity. At an early age Charles Spurgeon was influenced by his father and, in particular, his grandfather, both Nonconformist pastors. Reverend John Spurgeon (1810–1902), his father, was engaged in business in the week and ministered for sixteen years to the Congregational Church at Tollesbury each Sunday. John Spurgeon would, at a later date, pastor in Braintree and London. Spurgeon's grandfather, Reverend James Spurgeon (1776–1864), ministered for fifty-four years at the Stambourne Congregational (Independent) Church. He was a noted gospel preacher, a highly respected and esteemed man with a dry sense of humour.[3]

At an early age, Spurgeon stayed with his grandfather. His sharp mind and near photographic memory were evident to all. He absorbed himself with reading, in particular John Bunyan's *Pilgrim's Progress* and *Foxe's Book of Martyrs*. In his teenage years, Spurgeon immersed himself in Puritan theology, reading and understanding the best of the Puritans: John Owen (1616–1683), Richard Sibbes (1577–1635), John Flavel (1628–1691) and Matthew Henry (1662–1714). Spurgeon stood

---

3　W.Y. Fullerton, *Charles H. Spurgeon: London's Most Popular Preacher* (Chicago: Moody Press, 1966), 11–16.

out as a natural leader and an exceptional student, gifted with a sharp mind and a rare clarity of speech.[4]

God had his hand upon Spurgeon at an early age. Two events that took place are worthy of citation. First, the young zealous Spurgeon upon seeing his grandfather's sadness over the spiritual state of Mr. Roads, a member of the church at Stambourne, cried, "I'll kill old Roads, that I will!" Later on the young Spurgeon returned triumphantly and declared to his grandfather, "I've killed old Roads; he'll never grieve my grandpa anymore." James Spurgeon was astonished. Upon inquiry, Spurgeon boldly proclaimed, "I haven't been doing any harm, grandpa," said the child; "I've been about the Lord's work, that's all."[5] Later, Mr. Roads appeared at the parsonage with a downcast look and asked Spurgeon's grandfather for forgiveness, saying he would never backslide again. Mr. Roads then informed the grandfather what had happened:

> I'm very sorry indeed, my dear pastor, to have caused you such grief and trouble.... I was a-sitting in the public [house] just having my pipe and mug of beer, when that child comes in—to think an old man like me should be took to task, and reproved by a child like that! Well, he points at me with his finger, just so, and says, "What doest thou here Elijah? Sitting with the ungodly; and you a member of a church, and breaking your pastor's heart. I'm ashamed of you! I wouldn't break my pastor's heart I'm sure."[6]

Spurgeon, even at a tender age, displayed a gospel zeal for God's glory flamed with pathos that would characterize his future lifelong gospel ministry.

The second noteworthy event was when Rev. Richard Knill (1787–1857) a former missionary to India and well-esteemed minister was visiting Rev. James Spurgeon at the parsonage. Rev. Knill was so

---

4   Susannah Spurgeon and Joseph Harrald, *C.H. Spurgeon's Autobiography: Compiled from His Diary, Letters and Records 1834–1892*, 4 vols. (1897–1900; reprint, 4 vols. in 2, Pasadena, Texas: Pilgrim Publications, 1992), 1:23.

5   *Autobiography*, 1:23–24.

6   *Autobiography*, 1:23–24.

strangely drawn to the young Spurgeon that he went to his room and woke him up at six o'clock in the morning. He took the young boy into the parsonage garden and there Rev. Knill spoke directly into the young boy's heart. Spurgeon warmly recalls, "...he told me of the love of Jesus and of the blessedness of trusting in Him and loving Him in our childhood." Spurgeon affectionately comments, "With many a story he preached Christ to me and told me how good God had been to him, and then he prayed that I might know the Lord and serve Him." This continued for three days. Just before his departure, all the family gathered for morning prayer. Rev. Knill placed the boy on his knees and uttered this now famous prophecy, "This child will one day preach the Gospel, and he will preach it to great multitudes. I am persuaded that he will preach in the chapel of Rowland Hill."[7] Spurgeon recalls he spoke very solemnly and asked the boy to learn and use William Cowper's (1731–1800) hymn, "God moves in a mysterious way," on the occasion.[8] This prophecy was indeed fulfilled, and it perhaps influenced Spurgeon's own belief and openness to a "word of knowledge" in his own pulpit ministry.[9]

Conversion

Spurgeon's conversion was to be the great turning point in his life. At age fifteen, while Spurgeon was going to church in Colchester, Essex, a snowstorm intercepted him. He turned down a side street into a Primitive Methodist Chapel. In that chapel were perhaps fifteen people. The preacher for the day was "snowed up," so another person preached. Speculations on the date and the preacher have been presented in numerous biographies. However, in the editorial footnote[10] the date is clearly stated: "It is definitely known that the date of Mr. Spurgeon's conversion was January 6, 1850, for preaching at New Park Street Chapel, on Lord's-day morning January 6, 1856, from Isaiah 45:22, he said that six years before, that very day, and at that very hour,

---

7 *Autobiography*, 1:33–35.

8 For further details including later correspondence between Knill and Spurgeon consult *Autobiography*, 1:34–38.

9 *Autobiography*, 1:34–35.

10 *Autobiography*, 1:108.

he had been led to look to Christ, by a sermon from that text." However, speculation continues to abound as to the name of the preacher who was used of God to preach the gospel to C.H. Spurgeon.[11] Most biographies are silent, others add to the speculation. However, in an unpublished dissertation,[12] Timothy McCoy carefully evaluates the evidence and states, "First, a candid appraisal of the facts seems to leave little doubt that Robert Eaglen was the preacher of the famous 'Look' sermon. His own testimony combined with that of Robert Taylor, Joshua Elsden, and John Bloomfield is quite persuasive." If this is so, a question arises as to why Spurgeon, who met Eaglen later, did not recognize him. Timothy McCoy postulates three reasons. First, Robert Eaglen at the time of preaching had been emaciated with pulmonary consumption, but had recovered in both health and weight and, therefore, his appearance was very different. Second, the meeting was very brief, so brief in fact that Robert Eaglen never spoke. Third, Spurgeon perhaps desired to keep the instrument anonymous to ensure that God alone would be glorified, not the instrument he sovereignly chose to use.

The now famous text that God used to unveil the glory of Christ to Spurgeon and call him to himself was: "Look unto me, and be ye saved, all the ends of the earth" (Isaiah 45:22). Spurgeon vividly recalls how that sermon was etched into his heart:

> Look unto Me; I am sweatin' great drops of blood. Look unto Me; I am hangin' on a cross. Look unto Me; I am dead and buried. Look unto Me; I rise again. Look unto Me; I ascend to heaven. Look unto Me; I am sittin' at the Father's right hand. O poor sinner, look unto Me! Look unto Me![13]

After ten minutes or so, the preacher riveted his gaze on the young Spurgeon sitting under the gallery and cried:

---

11   See G. Holden Pike, *The Life and Work of Charles Haddon Spurgeon*, 6 vols. (1894; reprint, 6 vols. in 2, Edinburgh: The Banner of Truth Trust, 1991), 1:36.

12   Timothy Albert McCoy, "The Evangelistic Ministry of C.H. Spurgeon: Implications for a Contemporary Model for Pastoral Evangelism" (Unpublished Ph.D. thesis, The Southern Baptist Theological Seminary, 1989), 347–348.

13   *Autobiography*, 1:106.

"Young man, you look very miserable and you always will be miserable—miserable in life and in death, —if you don't obey my text; but if you obey now, this moment, you will be saved." Then, lifting up his hands, he shouted as only a Primitive Methodist could do, "Young man look to Jesus Christ. Look! Look! Look! You have nothin' to do but to look and live."[14]

Spurgeon writes, "I saw at once the way of salvation.... Oh! I looked until I could almost have looked my eyes away... I could have risen that instant, and sung with the most enthusiastic of them, of the precious blood of Christ, and the simple faith which looks alone to Him."[15]

At the tender age of fifteen years old, Spurgeon looked and lived. His life, like his ancestors before him, would now be completely given over to the gospel of Christ Jesus. Arnold Dallimore, in his excellent biography on C.H. Spurgeon, perceptively points out that Spurgeon's gospel ministry was shaped by the events that led to his conversion: "The failure of preachers he had heard to present the gospel, and to do so in a plain, direct manner, caused him throughout his whole ministry to tell sinners in every sermon and in a most forthright and understandable way how to be saved."[16]

A few days later Spurgeon penned in his diary a signed covenant between himself and his God entitled, "Consecration":

O great and unsearchable God, who knowest my heart, and triest all my ways; with a humble dependence upon the support of Thy Holy Spirit, I yield up myself to Thee; as Thy own reasonable sacrifice, I return to Thee Thine own. I would be forever, unreservedly, perpetually Thine; whilst I am on earth, I would serve Thee; and may I enjoy Thee and praise Thee forever! Amen. Feb. 1, 1850.[17]

---

14 *Autobiography*, 1:106.
15 *Autobiography*, 1:106.
16 Arnold Dallimore, Spurgeon (*Chicago*: Moody Press, 1984), 20.
17 *Autobiography*, 1:129.

Baptism

Spurgeon's due diligence in examining the Scriptures led him to break with his family's tradition as he became convicted about believer's baptism. Even at an early age, his mind and heart were captive to the Word of God. However, it was not an easy matter to break with family tradition for one with such a tender conscience. He wrote to his father from Newmarket on April 6, 1850, asking permission to be baptized in order to publicly proclaim Christ and take part in the Lord's table:

> My Dear Father.... Owing to my scruples on account of baptism, I did not sit down at the Lord's table, and cannot in conscience do so until I am baptised.... As Mr. Cantlow's baptising season will come around this month, I have humbly to beg your consent, as I will not act against your will, and should very much like to Commune next month. I have no doubt of your permission.[18]

Receiving no reply, the obedient yet anxious Spurgeon wrote to his mother a few weeks later on April 20: "My Dear Mother, I have every morning looked for a letter from Father, I long for an answer; it is now a month since I had one from him. Do if you please, send me either permission or refusal to be baptised; I have been kept in painful suspense."[19]

Eventually parental permission was given, albeit reluctantly, and Charles Spurgeon was baptized on his mother's birthday, May 3, 1850, by a Baptist minister, W.W. Cantlow of Isleham, a village some eight miles from Newmarket. The River Lark bore witness to Spurgeon's obedience to his Lord's command. He pens in his diary: "Blest pool! Sweet emblem to my death to all the world!"[20] Spurgeon describes the experience and the blessing of boldness to declare the wonders of the gospel:

> I was up early, to have a couple of hours of quiet prayer and dedication to God. Then I had some eight miles to walk.... The wind

---

18 *Autobiography*, 1:121.
19 *Autobiography*, 1:122.
20 *Autobiography*, 1:135.

John Spurgeon
(1810-1902)

blew down the river with a cutting blast… I felt as if Heaven and earth, and hell, might all gaze upon me; for I was not ashamed, there and then, to own myself a follower of the Lamb. My timidity was washed away…. Baptism also loosed my tongue and from that day it has never been quiet. I lost a thousand fears in that River Lark, and found that "in keeping His commandments there is great reward."[21]

Like his father and his grandfather, Spurgeon's heart and soul were fixed on pastoral ministry. His evangelistic fervour now awakened, he vigorously pursued every opportunity to preach the gospel.

Spurgeon's ministry at Waterbeach

At the age of seventeen, Spurgeon received a call to pastor a small Baptist church in the village of Waterbeach, a tiny hamlet northeast of Cambridge. While travelling through the village, Spurgeon's heart was burdened for souls. He wrote, "How earnestly do I wish that my life may be spent in lighting one soul after another with the sacred flame of eternal life! I would myself be as much as possible unseen while at work, and would vanish into eternal brilliance above when my work is done."[22] God was pleased to grant Spurgeon his heart's desire. Within a few months, Waterbeach was transformed and the little thatched chapel filled to overflowing. His first and last sermons at Waterbeach were from the text: "Thou shalt call his name Jesus, for He will save His people from their sins" (Matthew 1:21).[23] He laboured faithfully there from the autumn 1851 to April 1854. God blessed his efforts, and within two years the membership had more than doubled from forty to one hundred. Spurgeon believed it was here that God placed his seal of approval upon his ministry. Before Spurgeon arrived, the small community was filled with drunkenness and profanity, riot and iniquity. Commenting on his ministry in Waterbeach, Spurgeon writes:

---

21 *Autobiography*, 1:151–152.
22 *Autobiography*, 1:227.
23 *Autobiography*, 1:229.

It pleased the Lord to work signs and wonders in our midst. He showed the power of Jesus' name, and made us witnesses of that Gospel which can win souls, draw reluctant hearts, and mould the life and conduct of men afresh.[24]

Pastoral call to New Park Street Chapel

New Park Street Baptist Church in London soon heard of the young Spurgeon and invited him to preach. Because of the church's prestigious history,[25] Spurgeon's initial response to their invitation was that they must have the wrong Spurgeon, for he was a mere youth at nineteen![26] In Spurgeon's day, the church had lost its former glory and was now poorly located in a deteriorating neighbourhood with many warehouses surrounding it.

His first sermon, delivered on December 18, 1853, on a cold winter morning, was titled "The Father of Light," based on James 1:17. Spurgeon spoke with great freedom and boldness, as one convinced that he had a message from God. Moreover, he was experienced; although a youth, he had already preached 673 sermons.[27] In a letter to his father, Spurgeon writes that the congregation was Calvinistic and longed for the gospel to be preached with unction rather than some learned discourse from college men. Many, he wrote, thought that he was John Rippon over again.[28]

His initial reception was mixed. Spurgeon was invited back for a number of preaching engagements (January 1, 15 and 29, 1854), but before the final date, the church had taken definite action and issued a unanimous call.[29] The humbled Spurgeon accepted the call but asked

---

24 Ernest W. Bacon, *Spurgeon: Heir of the Puritans* (London: George Allen & Unwin, 1967), 32.

25 For a historical sketch of New Park Street Chapel, consult R. Shindler, *From the Usher's Desk to the Tabernacle Pulpit: The Life and Labours of Pastor C.H. Spurgeon* (London: Passmore and Alabaster, 1892), 71–84; the church had had a string of outstanding pastors, for instance, Benjamin Keach (1668 to 1704), John Gill (1720 to 1771) and John Rippon (1773 to 1836).

26 *Autobiography*, 1:317.

27 *Autobiography*, 1:321.

28 *Autobiography*, 1:340–341.

29 *Autobiography*, 1:344–345.

for a three-month trial period. His humility can be clearly seen in his acceptance letter, written when he was just nineteen years of age. The letter is set forth in full since it reveals his already rich understanding of pastoral ministry:

75 Dover Road, Borough,
April 28th, 1854.

TO THE BAPTIST CHURCH OF CHRIST WORSHIPPING
IN NEW PARK STREET CHAPEL, SOUTHWARK

DEARLY-BELOVED IN CHRIST JESUS,
I have received your unanimous invitation, as contained in a resolution passed by you on the 19th inst., desiring me to accept the pastorate among you. No lengthened reply is required: I ACCEPT IT. I have not been perplexed as to what my reply should be, for many things constrain me thus to answer.

I sought not to come to you, for I was the minister of an obscure but affectionate people; I never solicited advancement. The first note of invitation came from your deacons quite unlooked for, and I trembled at the idea of preaching in London... I would wish to give myself into the hands of our covenant God, whose wisdom directs all things. He shall choose for me; and as far as I can judge, this is His choice.

I feel it to be a high honour to be the Pastor of a people who can mention glorious names as my predecessors, and I entreat of you to remember me in prayer, that I may realize the solemn responsibility of my trust. Remember my youth and inexperience; pray that these may not hinder my usefulness. I trust also that the remembrance of these may lead you to forgive the mistakes I may make, or unguarded words I may utter.

Blessed be the name of the Most High! If He has called me to this office, He will support me in it, otherwise how should a child, a youth, have the presumption thus to attempt a work that filled the heart and hands of Jesus? Your kindness to me has been very great, and my heart is knit unto you. I fear not for your steadfastness, I fear my own.... Oh, that I may be no injury to you, but a lasting benefit! I have no more to say, only this, that if I have expressed myself in these few words in a manner unbecoming my youth and inexperience, you will not impute it to arrogance, but forgive my mistake.

And now, commending you to our covenant-keeping God, the Triune Jehovah,

I am.

Yours to serve in the Gospel,

C.H. SPURGEON.[30]

Interestingly, Mr. Sheridan Knowles, the celebrated playwright and actor, an instructor in elocution at Stepney, now Regent's Park College, was so awestruck with Spurgeon that he urged all his students to hear him preach! Mr. Knowles made this prophetic utterance to his students concerning Spurgeon:

Now, mark my word, boys, that young man will live to be the greatest preacher of this or any other age. He will bring more souls to Christ than any other man who ever proclaimed the gospel, not excepting the apostle Paul. His name will be known everywhere, and his Sermons will be translated into many languages of the world.[31]

Within a few months of his arrival at New Park Street Baptist Church, Spurgeon was hailed as "a second Whitefield." The attendance rocketed from 200 to well over 1,000. The fame of Spurgeon rapidly spread across England and, alas, so did his critics. Spurgeon often found himself caricatured in the cruellest of ways. However, God used this for good, for many came with curiosity and scorn only to find Christ. Spurgeon writes: "Men and women had come in, out of curiosity, —a curiosity often created by some unfounded story, or malicious slander of prejudiced minds; yet Jesus Christ has called them, and they became both His disciples and our warm-hearted friends."[32]

---

30 *Autobiography*, 1:352–353.
31 *Autobiography*, 1:354.
32 *Autobiography*, 1:365.

Spurgeon attributed this success and the success of his lifelong ministry to the prayers of God's people. Spurgeon was convinced that the church prayer meeting was the key to ministerial success:

> When I came to New Park Street Chapel, it was but a mere handful of people to whom I first preached; yet I can never forget how earnestly they prayed. Sometimes they seemed to plead as though they could really see the Angel of the covenant present with them, as if they must have a blessing from Him. More than once, we were so awe-struck with the solemnity of the meeting, that we sat silent for some moments while the Lord's power appeared to overshadow us…[33]

This glorious experience would bring a lifelong conviction to Spurgeon that gospel preaching found its blessing and success in the prayers of God's people.

Surrey Gardens Music Hall

The growing crowds needed to be accommodated so Spurgeon looked to the Surrey Gardens Music Hall (it could seat 10,000). Soon, however, one event would strike a tragic note into the young preacher's heart. At the Music Hall one evening, someone cried, "Fire! The galleries are giving way, the place is falling." Panic immediately broke out. People rushed to the doors, some fell and were trampled, the stair railing broke under the pressure, and people toppled over. Twenty-eight people were taken to hospital; sadly, seven lost their lives. Not knowing what had taken place, Spurgeon tried to preach. Upon realizing what had happened, Spurgeon fainted and was carried out. The place was in an uproar. Spurgeon returned home later that evening, a broken man. Upon entering his home, he knelt down at the sofa and wept. In the dark and difficult days that followed, Spurgeon, now a broken and depressed man, penned these words:

> Who can conceive the anguish of my sad spirit? I refused to be comforted: tears were my meat by day and dreams my terror at

---

33 *Autobiography*, 1:361.

Surrey Gardens Music Hall

night… My Bible, once my daily food, was but a hand to lift the sluices of my woe. Prayer yielded no balm to me.[34]

However, in the midst of trials and tears, he turned afresh to Christ. "Then did I cast my burden upon the Lord…. Scorn, tumult and war seemed less than nothing for His sake. I girded up my loins to run before His chariot and shout forth His glory."[35] After missing two Sundays, Spurgeon returned but switched the morning services to the Music Hall and the evening to Park Street Chapel. This continued for the next three years, from November 1856 to December 1859.

The Lord was pleased to bring triumph out of tragedy. Overnight, Spurgeon became a household name among the masses, and the crowds increased! One leading newspaper, reflecting on the catastrophe thirty years earlier, wrote, "Curious enough, it was an accident of a serious nature that first drew the attention of the world in general to the rising influence of Mr. Spurgeon."[36]

Metropolitan Tabernacle

In order to accommodate the large numbers, the Metropolitan Tabernacle was built at the Elephant and Castle, South London. Spurgeon would minister morning and evening each Sunday to around 6,000 people. Five thousand would be seated and another 1,000 would have to stand. There were numerous converts under his bold Christocentric preaching.

The congregation consisted of many lower-middle-class folk, many of them highly successful, godly people. However, there were also some from the upper classes. Among the more notable of the latter who attended at times were Lord John Russell, Lady Peel, Lord Shaftesbury, Lord Campbell, the Archbishop of Canterbury, Florence Nightingale, George Eliot, Matthew Arnold, Prime Minister William Gladstone (who sat in the pulpit behind him) and the young David Lloyd George, who would be appointed Prime Minister at a later date.[37]

---

34 W.Y. Fullerton, *Charles H. Spurgeon: London's Most Popular Preacher* (Chicago: Moody Press, 1966), 83–84.

35 Fullerton, *Spurgeon: London's Most Popular Preacher*, 84.

36 Fullerton, *Spurgeon: London's Most Popular Preacher*, 85.

37 Geoff Thomas, "The Preacher's Progress" in Erroll Hulse, ed., *A Marvellous*

During Spurgeon's entire pastorate, 14,700 people were added to the membership roll of the Metropolitan Tabernacle, 10,800 by baptism and the rest by transfer from other churches.[38]

Spurgeon's first sermon preached at the new Metropolitan Tabernacle was on March 31, 1861. It was called "Temple Glories," and his clear focus was on his sovereign Lord and the enabling of the Holy Spirit. He boldly declares:

> Let God send the fire of His Spirit here, and the minister will be more and more lost in his Master. You will come to think less of the minister and more of the truth spoken. … Suppose the fire should come here, and the Master be seen more than the minister, what then? Why, the church will become two, three and four thousand strong. … We shall have the lecture hall beneath this platform crowded at each prayer meeting, and we shall see in this place young men devoting themselves to God; we shall find ministers raised up, and trained and sent forth to carry the sacred fire to other parts of the globe. … If God shall bless us, He will make us a blessing to multitudes of others. Let God but send down the fire, and the biggest sinners in the neighbourhood will be converted; those who live in dens of infamy will be changed; the drunkard will forsake his cups, the swearer will repent of his blasphemy, the debauched will leave their lusts—
>
> Dry bones be raised, and clothed afresh,
> And hearts of stone be turned hearts of flesh.[39]

Spurgeon was very active in a number of ventures within the ministry of the church. His weekly printed sermons were read worldwide, which amounted to nearly one million readers. The publication of his sermons continued even after his death and numbered 3,561 (from

---

Ministry: How the All-Round Ministry of C.H. Spurgeon Speaks to Us Today (Darlington: Evangelical Press, 1993), 37–38.

38 Bacon, *Spurgeon: Heir of the Puritans*, 60.

39 "Temple Glories," *Metropolitan Tabernacle Pulpit* (reprint; Albany: AGES Software, 2000), 408.

1855 to 1917). He was the editor of *The Sword and the Trowel*, a monthly magazine put out by the Metropolitan Tabernacle. Spurgeon authored a number of books: *C.H. Spurgeon's Autobiography: Compiled from His Diary, Letters and Records* is largely his thoughts reworked by his wife and private secretary; *Lectures To My Students* and *An All-Round Ministry* are both filled with admonition for his ministerial students and alumni at the Pastors' College. (Spurgeon founded the Pastors' College in 1856 and over 900 students passed through its doors before his death.) *All of Grace* and *Around the Wicket Gate* were written for those seeking salvation; *According to Promise*, to explain God's providential dealings and *Faith's Cheque Book*, a daily devotional, to edify God's people. Several commentaries, including *The Treasury of David*, *The Gospel of the Kingdom. A Popular Exposition of The Gospel According to Matthew* and *Commenting & Commentaries*, which was written to guide pastors in their choice of commentators, to name but a few. Spurgeon also organized two orphanages, as well as numerous other institutions (estimates run at sixty in total).

Theological sketch

Spurgeon openly declared, "My daily labour is to revive the old doctrines of Gill, Owen, Calvin, Augustine and Christ."[40] He tenaciously upheld what are called "the doctrines of grace," and because of this he proclaimed a sovereign God who is Lord in salvation, one who is calling out his elect people through the atoning work of Jesus Christ. Spurgeon felt Calvinism demonstrates beautifully how the belief in the sovereign, electing grace of God empowers the gospel and infuses zeal for evangelism. In fact, rather than hinder or diminish the gospel, Calvinism demonstrates the gospel's power in calling sinners to a Saviour. Calvinism declares the actuality of salvation as opposed to the Arminian gospel of potentiality. Spurgeon never hid his love for the doctrines of grace but proclaimed them unashamedly throughout his life and pulpit ministry. With characteristic humour, the young Spurgeon proclaimed in the Exeter Hall, Strand, on March 4, 1855:

---

40 Iain H. Murray, *The Forgotten Spurgeon* (Edinburgh: The Banner of Truth Trust, 1978), 58.

The doctrines of original sin, election, effectual call, final perseverance, and all those great truths which are called Calvinism…
are, I believe, the essential doctrines of the Gospel that is in Jesus
Christ. Now I do not ask you if you believe all this—it is possible,
you may not; but I believe you will before you enter heaven. I am
persuaded that as God may wash your hearts, he will wash your
brains before you enter heaven.[41]

Controversy sketch

Unlike some evangelists, Spurgeon not only proclaimed the gospel, but
he also defended the gospel. He never looked for a battle, but when it
came, he never sidestepped the issues like so many today. Four great
theological controversies erupted during Spurgeon's life.

First, as people began to read Spurgeon's printed sermons, controversy erupted over his Calvinism. He was not "hyper" enough for
some; he was too Calvinistic for others![42] Criticism abounded in the
religious pages of the newspapers, but Spurgeon kept his eyes on his
Saviour and preached on. Spurgeon wrote to a friend, "I am not easily
put down. I go on and care for no man on earth."[43]

Second, on June 5, 1864, Spurgeon, "Mr. Valiant-for-Truth,"[44]
preached against Baptismal regeneration from Mark 16:15–16.
Spurgeon believed that many would reject him and his ministry over
this controversial issue. However, the response was electrifying and
more of his sermons were purchased than ever before—a quarter of a
million! A hornet's nest was stirred up, and clergy all over England
wrote to either defend or attack Spurgeon. However, little was
achieved, the advocates of Baptismal regeneration continued on
their way, and Baptists took heart and were strengthened in their
position.[45] Spurgeon's humour was again evident in this matter: "I

---

41 "The Peculiar Sleep of the Beloved" in *The New Park Street Pulpit*, 6 vols. (1855–
1860; reprint, 6 vols. in 3, Pasadena: Pilgrim Publications, 1981), 1:92.

42 Consult Iain H. Murray, *Spurgeon v. Hyper-Calvinism: The Battle for Gospel Preaching* (Edinburgh: The Banner of Truth Trust, 1995), 39–124.

43 Cited in Warren Wiersbe, *Walking with the Giants: A Minister's Guide to Good
Reading and Great Preaching* (Grand Rapids: Baker Book House, 1976), 73.

44 A character in the second part of John Bunyan's *Pilgrim's Progress*.

45 Bacon, *Spurgeon: Heir of the Puritans*, 128.

hear you are in hot water," a friend said to him. "Oh, no," Spurgeon replied, "it is the other fellows who are in hot water. I am the stoker, the fellow that makes the water boil."[46]

Third, tension developed when another famous London preacher, Joseph Parker, pastor of City Temple, rather unwisely published an open letter to Spurgeon in the *British Weekly*, on April 25, 1890. Spurgeon's Pastor's Conference was being held the week it was published, making the vindictive article even more devastating. It said, in part:

> Let me advise you to widen the circle of which you are the centre. You are surrounded by offers of incense. They flatter your weaknesses, they laugh at your jokes, they feed you with compliments. My dear Spurgeon, you are too big a man for this. Take in more fresh air…scatter your ecclesiastical harem. I do not say destroy your circle: I simply say enlarge it…[47]

Fourth, the most painful theological controversy developed among Spurgeon's brethren in the Baptist Union (1887–1889). Robert Shindler, a close friend, anonymously published two articles in *The Sword and the Trowel* expressing concern over growing heresy in some Baptist churches. The first two articles were called "The Down Grade."[48] Spurgeon later writes:

> It now becomes a serious question how far those who abide by the faith once delivered to the saints should fraternize with those who have turned aside to another gospel. Christian love has its claims, and divisions are to be shunned as grievous evils; but how far are we justified in being in confederacy with those who are departing from the truth?[49]

---

46 Cited in Wiersbe, *Walking with the Giants*, 73.

47 Cited in Wiersbe, *Walking with the Giants*, 75–76.

48 Consult *The Down Grade Controversy: Collected Materials which Reveal the Viewpoint of the Late Charles Haddon Spurgeon … on one of the most significant disputes of his ministry* (Pasadena: Pilgrim Publications, 1978).

49 Cited in Wiersbe, *Walking with the Giants*, 74.

In the midst of controversy, Spurgeon struggled over the loss of friends, slander, rejection and isolation. His health began to break, but like many before him, and heir of the Puritans of another day, Spurgeon could not, would not, surrender the gospel. On October 28, 1887, the Metropolitan Tabernacle withdrew from the fellowship of the Baptist Union. With a heavy heart, Spurgeon writes, "Dear Friend, I beg to intimate to you, as the Secretary of the Baptist Union, that I must withdraw from the society.... I beg you not to send anyone to me to ask for reconsideration."[50]

Sermon sketch

In examining Spurgeon's sermons, we shall see that he was a great preacher and expounder of the cross. John A. Broadus (1827–1895) and D. L. Moody (1837–1899) greatly admired Spurgeon for his gospel preaching. *The Daily Telegraph*, a leading newspaper of the day, commented on Spurgeon's pulpit power on January 14, 1888:

> As a pulpit orator he had special advantages. He had a voice of marvellous power, penetration, and variety of tone.... He had resources, readily drawn upon, of pathos and a certain kind of humour; and he could vivify his sermons by all manner of telling and homely, sometimes perhaps too homely, illustrations. He never preached over his listeners or at them. He always talked directly to them. He was always intensely in earnest. His emotions carried himself, as well as his congregation, away.[51]

Spurgeon the Calvinist, from his lips and heart, pleaded with sinners to be reconciled to God. Although he holds tenaciously to a sovereign God, he pleads for souls to respond. This is how he concludes his sermon on April 7, 1867, at the Agricultural Hall, Islington:

> Oh come, ye needy, come to my Master! Ho, ye that have been disappointed with rites and ceremonies, and feelings, and impressions, and all of the hopes of the flesh, come at my Master's

---

50 Pike, *The Life and Works of Charles Haddon Spurgeon*, 6:287.
51 Fullerton, *Spurgeon: London's Most Popular Preacher*, 86.

command, and look up to Him! He is not here in the flesh; for He is risen; but He has risen to plead for sinners, and "He is able to save them to the uttermost that come unto God by Him, seeing He ever liveth to make intercession for them." Oh, if I could know how to preach the gospel so that you would feel it, I would go to any school to learn! The Lord knows I would willingly consent to lose these eyes, to get greater power in my ministry; ay, and to lose arms, legs, and all my members. I would be willing to die if I could be honoured by the Holy Spirit to win this mass of souls to God.[52]

Twenty-eight years later, Spurgeon continued to yearn to see souls won to the Saviour. In a sermon preached on July 10, 1887, from the pulpit at the Metropolitan Tabernacle—less than five years before his death—Spurgeon still longs to see fruit for his labours as he pleads for sinners to seek eternal life:

Oh, that I knew how to bring you to Christ, dear hearers! This is a hot summer's night, and you are weary, perhaps, of my talking; but I would not mind that if I could bring you to Jesus. Oh, that I might have fruit from this sermon also! This week, I believe I might say that I have met and heard of hundreds who, in past years, have been brought to the Saviour by the printed sermons. They came to me, grasped my hand, and thanked me, and I praised God; but then I thought, "Yes, God did bless me, and He has blessed the printed sermons; but I want present fruit, and to see sinners now close in with Christ, and be eternally saved.... if I only tell you of a true salvation, and a true Saviour, come and have it, come and trust Him now, for He casts out none who come to Him. May this be the deciding time with many of you, for our Lord Jesus Christ's sake! Amen.[53]

---

52 "Jesus at Bethesda" in *Metropolitan Tabernacle Pulpit*, 63 vols. (1856–1904; reprint, Pasadena: Pilgrim Publication, 1979), 13:204.

53 "The Model Soul Winner" in *Metropolitan Tabernacle Pulpit*, 41:356.

Little wonder, Spurgeon comments, that the root cause of many useless ministries lies in the lack of distinctly recognizing the power of the Holy Ghost. A remarkable illustration of Spurgeon's own dependence on the Spirit in the pulpit is found in his *Autobiography*. Discussing instances of striking conversions under his preaching ministry, he relates that on one occasion he deliberately pointed to a man in the congregation and said:

"There is a man sitting there, who is a shoemaker; he keeps his shop open on Sundays, it was open last Sabbath morning, he took ninepence, and there was fourpence profit out of it; his soul is sold to Satan for fourpence!"

A city missionary, when going his rounds, met with this man, and seeing that he was reading one of my sermons, he asked the question, "Do you know Mr. Spurgeon?" "Yes," replied the man, "I have every reason to know him, I have been to hear him; and, under his preaching, by God's grace I have become a new creature in Christ Jesus. Shall I tell you how it happened? I went to the Music Hall, and took my seat in the middle of the place; Mr. Spurgeon looked at me as if he knew me, and in his sermon he pointed to me, and told the congregation that I was a shoemaker, and that I kept my shop open on Sundays; and I did, sir. I should not have minded that; but he also said that I took ninepence the Sunday before, and there was fourpence profit out of it. I did take ninepence that day, and fourpence was just the profit; but how he should know that, I could not tell. Then it struck me that it was God who had spoken to my soul through him, so I shut up my shop the next Sunday. At first, I was afraid to go again to hear him, lest he should tell the people more about me; but afterwards I went, and the Lord met with me, and saved my soul."[54]

Spurgeon went on to say that there were as "many as a dozen similar cases" in which he pointed at somebody in the Music Hall "without having the slightest knowledge of the person, or any idea that what I said was right, except that I believed I was moved by the Spirit to say

---

54 *Autobiography*, 2:226–227.

it; and so striking has been my description, that the persons have gone away, and said to their friends, "Come, see a man that told me all things that ever I did; beyond a doubt, he must have been sent of God to my soul, or else he could not have described me so exactly."[55]

Conclusion

We have seen that Spurgeon's spirituality shaped his life and empowered his ministry. Like many Baptist leaders before him, Spurgeon tenaciously believed in the Word of God. He left Baptists with a rich Calvinistic heritage exemplified in the best of gospel preaching. Spurgeon unashamedly preached Christ crucified. Moreover, his sermons are rich in theology, eloquence, compassion and urgency. He also preached for a decision as he expounded the cross and lifted high his Saviour. In addition, unlike some, he saw the imperative to defend the gospel against the inroads of Modernism, Roman Catholicism and cults.

We close this brief overview of God's choice servant by citing a stanza from the closing hymn of Spurgeon's final service here on earth. He chose to close with the Puritan Samuel Rutherford (c.1600–1661), not knowing that within two weeks he would gaze upon the face of his dearly loved Saviour:

> The sands of time are sinking,
>   The dawn of heaven breaks,
> The summer morn I've sighed for,
>   The fair, sweet morn awakes,
> Dark, dark has been the midnight,
>   But dayspring is at hand,
> And glory, glory dwelleth
>   In Emmanuel's land.[56]

Charles Haddon Spurgeon was called into the presence of his King on January 31, 1892, in Menton, France. The memorial and funeral services were held at the Metropolitan Tabernacle from February 7 to 11, 1892, and his body was laid to rest in West Norwood Cemetery,

---

55 *Autobiography*, 2:227. Verse referenced is John 4:29.
56 *Autobiography*, 4:370.

*The front of Spurgeon's crypt at West Norwood
Cemetery, South London*

South London. At the head and foot of the olive casket were plates bearing the following inscription: "I have fought a good fight, I have finished my course, I have kept the faith".[57]

The eulogy fell to Pastor Archibald G. Brown (1844–1922) of East London Tabernacle, a close ministerial friend and former graduate of the Pastors' College. With great pathos and many pauses, Brown declared:

> Beloved President, Faithful Pastor, Prince of Preachers, Brother Beloved, Dear Spurgeon—We bid thee not "farewell" but only for a little while "good-night." Thou shall rise soon, at the first dawn of the resurrection day of the redeemer. … Hard Worker in the field, thy toil is ended! No looking back has marred thy course. Harvests have followed thy patient sowing, and heaven is already rich with thine ingathered sheathes, and shall be still enriched through years yet lying in eternity. Champion of God, thy battle long and nobly fought is over. The sword, which clave to thy hand, has dropped at last; the palm branch takes its place. No longer does the helmet press thy brow, oft weary with its surging thoughts of battle; the victor's wreath from the Great Commander's hand has already proved thy full reward. Here, for a little while, shall rest thy precious dust. Then shall thy Wellbeloved come, and at His voice thou shalt spring from thy couch of earth, fashioned like unto His glorious body. Then spirit, soul, and body shall magnify thy Lord's redemption. Until then, beloved sleep! We praise God for thee; and, by the blood of the everlasting covenant, we hope and expect to praise God with thee. Amen."[58]

---

57 *Autobiography*, 4:370.
58 *Autobiography*, 4:375–376.

2

John Bunyan's life, ministry and spirituality

The influence of John Bunyan

This sketch of the life and ministry of John Bunyan (1628–1688) will set the stage for showing how this preacher from Bedfordshire had a lasting and significant impact, more than any other Baptist, on the life, thought and ministry of Charles Haddon Spurgeon. Bunyan's writing and preaching reveal a dread of sin and earnest and zealous lifelong pursuit of personal spirituality, which became a model for Spurgeon to follow. Bunyan's personal conviction that ministerial success finds its roots in a minister's personal spirituality deeply influenced the life and ministry of Spurgeon.

Historical background

John Bunyan was a Nonconformist who suffered a lengthy persecution for his faith. Yet, this preacher impacted the Christian community of his world and shaped Baptist heritage for many generations.

Bunyan was born into a land that was undergoing political and religious turmoil. A.R. Buckland points out that not long before Bunyan's birth the English Bible was only 100 years old, the Spanish Armada was in the memory of many and Elizabeth's great reign occurred less than twenty-five years prior.[1]

In the political arena, conflict raged between the Royalists and the Roundheads, which eventually developed into two civil wars (1642–1646; 1648–1649). In the religious arena, the Church of England faced internal turmoil from the Puritans who longed for reform. The Act of Uniformity (1662) was an attempt to bring control, but instead resulted in the ejection of 2,000 godly Puritan preachers, the cream of the Anglican church. This was the catalyst that helped forge the Nonconformist movement, which was composed mainly of Presbyterians, Congregationalists and Baptists. The Five Mile Act, another attempt to control the Nonconformists, soon followed in October 1665, which made outlaws of their preachers if they preached within a five-mile radius of a town. This act, passed in Oxford due to the bubonic plague in London, banished many pastors to obscure places and deprived them of a livelihood.

Yet in the midst of this political and religious turmoil, God raised up a number of spiritual giants, such men as Richard Sibbes, James Ussher (1581–1656), Alexander Henderson (1583–1646), Samuel Rutherford, Richard Baxter (1615–1691), John Owen, John Howe (1630–1705) and, standing tall among these giants of the faith, John Bunyan.

Bunyan's birth

Bunyan was born in 1628 at the village of Elstow, about one mile from Bedford. His parents were both poor and uneducated, yet they made sure that John received at least a basic school education. John Bunyan was christened at Elstow Parish Church on November 30, 1628. At the age of sixteen, Bunyan joined the Cromwellian army, under the godly influence of Oliver Cromwell (1599–1658). He probably served for a number of years. This experience would fuel his quill many years later.

Bunyan's personality and appearance

Regarding Bunyan's personality, appearance and growing popularity, Austen Kennedy de Blois gives some insight:

---

1   A.R. Buckland, *John Bunyan: The Man and His Work* (London: The Religious Tract Society, 1928), 15.

He is not a person to be overlooked. Though somewhat rough in outward seeming he has a commanding presence and an attractive personality. He has walked thirteen miles to this service. He is a man of rude health and abounding vitality.... He is unlearned, great-hearted, simple and eloquent of speech, a man of the people but already marked as a leader.... The very name of the man has drawn people here tonight. The announcement has gone from lip to lip and from house to house that he is to be the preacher, and when this preacher preaches, the crowds are drawn into fellowship, for the mighty fervour of the Lord God of hosts is upon him, and his words lay hold of people's hearts.[2]

There were five major turning points in Bunyan's life: his conversion, his call to ministry, his preaching, his imprisonment and his ongoing pursuit of spirituality.

Bunyan's conversion

Bunyan's early life was one of ungodliness, especially lust and profane language. He writes: "Being filled with all unrighteousness.... Cursing, swearing, lying, and blaspheming the holy name of God."[3] The fear of judgement and eternal hell provoked numerous nightmares for Bunyan. As a soldier under Cromwell, Bunyan was faced with the brevity of life when someone replaced him and was killed. He writes, "...but when I was just ready to go, one of the company desired to go in my room; to which when I had consented, he took my place; and coming to the siege, as he stood as sentinel, he was shot in the head with a musket bullet, and died."[4]

Shortly thereafter, Bunyan married a godly woman who, although poor, brought into the marriage two books that Bunyan would read from time to time: *The Plain Man's Pathway to Heaven* by Arthur Dent and *The Practice of Piety* by Lewis Bayly. Bunyan soon became "religious."

---

2 Austen Kennedy de Blois, *John Bunyan the Man* (Philadelphia: Judson Press, 1928), 3.

3 John Bunyan, *Grace Abounding to the Chief of Sinners* in George Offor, ed., *The Works of John Bunyan*, 3 vols. (Glasgow: Blackie and Son, 1860), 1:6.

4 *Grace Abounding to the Chief of Sinners*, *The Works of John Bunyan*, 1:7.

One particular Sunday, he recalls that the parson spoke on Sabbath breaking. At first, Bunyan thought the parson crafted the sermon with him in mind! The sermon hit hard and pricked Bunyan's conscience, "…so went home when the sermon was ended, with a great burden upon my spirit."[5] Soon after, he was back to his old profane ways, when he felt a question being impressed upon his heart: "Wilt thou leave thy sins and go to heaven, or have thy sins and go to hell?"[6]

A month later, Bunyan returned to his old ways—until rebuked by a loose and ungodly woman for his profanity! Bunyan reformed, but was not awakened. He tried to establish his own righteousness but was ignorant of the gospel. A year later, in the providential mercies of God, Bunyan overheard three or four women talking about the things of God. Bunyan was moved. He writes,

> …their talk was about a new birth, the work of God on their hearts, also how they were convinced of their miserable state by nature; they talked how God had visited their souls with his love in the Lord Jesus…and did contemn, slight, and abhor their own righteousness…as filthy and insufficient to do them any good. And methought they spake as if joy did make them speak; they spake with such pleasantness of Scripture language, and with such appearance of grace in all they said, that they were to me, as if they had found a new world. At this I felt my own heart begin to shake.[7]

Bunyan meditated upon these words and often returned to continue listening. He began in earnest to search the Scriptures. He went through much agony of soul.

One day he heard someone preaching on "Behold thou art fair, my love; behold thou art fair" (Song of Songs 4:1). Bunyan writes,

> Now was my heart filled full of comfort and hope, and now I could believe that my sins should be forgiven me; yea, I was now

5   *Grace Abounding to the Chief of Sinners, The Works of John Bunyan*, 1:8.

6   *Grace Abounding to the Chief of Sinners, The Works of John Bunyan*, 1:8.

7   *Grace Abounding to the Chief of Sinners, The Works of John Bunyan*, 1:9.

so taken with the love and mercy of God that I remember I could not tell how to contain till I got home; I thought, I could have spoken of His love and of His mercy to me even to the very crows that sat upon the ploughed lands before me...⁸

Bunyan's call to preach

Bunyan's call to preaching was central to his life and work. Above everything else, Bunyan, like other Puritans, was a preacher of the gospel. Bunyan describes his call to the ministry in great detail:

> Wherefore, though of myself, of all the great saints the most unworthy, yet I, but with great fear and trembling at the sight of my own weakness, did set upon the work, and did according to my gift, and the proportion of my faith, preach that blessed gospel that God had shown me in the holy Word of truth; which, when the country understood, they came in to hear the Word by hundreds, and that from all parts, though upon sundry and diverse accounts. And I thank God he gave unto me some measure of bowels and pity for their souls, which also did put me forward to labour with great diligence and earnestness, to find out such a word as might, if God would bless it, lay hold of, and awaken the conscience, in which also the good Lord had respect to the desire of his servant.⁹

Bunyan goes on to be amazed that God would use such a vessel as he:

> Indeed, I have been as one sent to them from the dead; I went myself in chains to preach to them in chains; and carried that fire in my own conscience that I persuade them to beware of. I can truly say, and that without dissembling, that when I have been to preach, I have gone full of guilt and terror even to the pulpit door, and there it had been taken off and I have been at liberty in my mind until I have done my work, and then imme-

---

8 *Grace Abounding to the Chief of Sinners, The Works of John Bunyan*, 1:17.
9 *Grace Abounding to the Chief of Sinners, The Works of John Bunyan*, 1:40–41.

diately, even before I could get down the pulpit stairs, I have been as bad as I was before; yet God carried me on, but surely with a strong hand, for neither guilt or hell could take me off my work.[10]

John Piper summarizes the power and influence of John Bunyan's preaching:

He would not be licensed as pastor of the Bedford church until seventeen years later. But his popularity as a powerful lay preacher exploded. The extent of his work grew. "When the country understood that…the tinker had turned preacher," John Brown tells us, "they came to hear the word by hundreds, and that from all parts. Charles Doe, a comb maker in London, said (later in Bunyan's life), "Mr. Bunyan preached so New Testament-like he made me admire and weep for joy, and give him my affections." In the days of toleration, a day's notice would get a crowd of 1,200 to hear him preach at seven o'clock on a weekday morning.

Once, while Bunyan was in prison, a whole congregation of sixty people was arrested and brought in at night. A witness tells us, "I…heard Mr. Bunyan both preach and pray with that mighty spirit of Faith and Plerophory [fulness] of Divine Assistance that…made me stand and wonder." John Owen, the greatest Puritan theologian and contemporary of John Bunyan, was once asked by King Charles why he, a great scholar, went to hear an uneducated tinker preach. He said, "I would willingly exchange my learning for the tinker's power of touching men's hearts.[11]

Bunyan's imprisonment

When Oliver Cromwell died on September 3, 1658, John Bunyan was thirty years old. Charles II was summoned from Breda, Holland, on the understanding that he would agree to religious liberty. Once

---

10 *Grace Abounding to the Chief of Sinners, The Works of John Bunyan*, 1:42.

11 John Piper, "Suffering and the Sovereignty of God" in *The Southern Baptist Journal of Theology*, vol. 4, No 2 (2000), 10. See also, John Piper, *The Hidden Smile of God: The Fruit of Affliction in the Lives of John Bunyan, William Cowper, and David Brainerd* (Wheaton, Illinois: Crossway Books, 2001), 53–54.

crowned, however, the tables were turned and religious persecution aimed at the Nonconformists broke out. Ultimatums were soon issued: conformity or imprisonment. Bunyan refused to stop preaching and was therefore sent to prison. Ironically, persecution actually strengthened the cause it sought to slay. Citing two English and two Scottish Nonconformists, Marcus L. Loane points out the real issue was that Bunyan and others were in fact fighting for religious liberty:

> These four men [Alexander Henderson, Samuel Rutherford, John Bunyan and Richard Baxter] were all in the van of the freedom-fighters in their own age, and they fought for freedom of truth and conscience, freedom for life and worship, freedom both as citizens and as Christians…. They were fired by an inner nobility of motive and ideal which lifts them far above petty criticism and gives them a lasting title to be known as men who were like Bunyan's pilgrim, Valiant-for-Truth.[12]

Vera Brittain also writes, "He is the individual who established, through political confusion and religious persecution, the right to maintain a direct relationship between himself and God. To him we owe that freedom of worship which the English-speaking world, unlike other nations of our day, has never forfeited."[13] She further points out the maturing nature of Bunyan's confinement, from a short-tempered young man to one of growing maturity. She writes, "John Bunyan went into Bedford County Gaol a hot-headed young rebel just thirty-two years old. He came out a mature and experienced man of forty-three, in whose presence other prisoners had died."[14]

While in Bedford prison, Bunyan wrote *Pilgrim's Progress*, a wonderful analogy of the pursuit of holiness. In the prison, while facing numerous hardships and periods of relative freedom, Bunyan was not idle. During his twelve years in Bedford jail, Bunyan wrote numerous

---

12 Marcus L. Loane, *Makers of Puritan History* (Grand Rapids: Eerdmans Publishing Company, 1961), 12.

13 Vera Brittain, *In the Steps of John Bunyan: An Excursion into Puritan England* (London: Rich and Cowan, 1950), 15.

14 Brittain, *In the Steps of John Bunyan*, 14.

books: *Profitable Meditations* (1661), *Prayer* [*I will Pray in the Spirit*] (1663), *Christian Behaviour* (1663), *One Thing Needful* (1665), *The Holy City* (1665), *Resurrection of the Dead* (1665) and *Grace Abounding to the Chief of Sinners* (1666).[15] Perhaps, his confinement was the pinnacle of his ministry for there he began to write *Pilgrim's Progress*, which shaped countless lives—including C.H. Spurgeon's—for generations.

Bunyan's pursuit of personal spirituality

Bunyan's heart and passion for personal spirituality is summed up in his discourse entitled, "A Holy Life: The Beauty of Christianity." The discourse is an exposition of 2 Timothy 2:19. This original work was published in 1684 but became so rare that previous editors of Bunyan's works missed it until it was republished in 1780. Here we see Bunyan's great insight to the subtleties of sin and its terror. For example, in the introduction, Bunyan points out that there is a difference between true faith and false faith in that one seeks holiness in all aspects, while the other picks and chooses the easiest path. True faith will be evidenced in the pursuit of holiness in all aspects as it seeks to obey. Bunyan rightly points out:

> There are works that cost nothing, and works that are chargeable. And observe it, the unsound faith will choose to itself the most easy works it can find. For example, there is reading, praying, hearing of sermons, baptism, breaking of bread, church fellowship, preaching, and the like; and there is mortification of lusts, charity, simplicity, open-heartedness, with a liberal hand to the poor, and their like also. Now the unsound faith picks and chooses, and takes and leaves, but the true faith does not so.[16]

As Bunyan expounds on this theme, he cites eight points to encourage his readers to pursue holiness by rejecting sin:

15 Edward E. Hindson, *Introduction to Puritan Theology* (Grand Rapids: Baker Book House, 1976), 221–222.

16 *The Works of John Bunyan*, 2:508.

John Bunyan
(1628–1688)

1. *Remember* that God sees thee, and has his eyes open upon thee…
2. *Remember* that God's wrath abides against [sin], and that he will surely be revenged on it, and on all that gives it entertainment.
3. *Remember* the mischiefs that it has done to those who have embraced it and what distress it has brought upon others.
4. *Remember* that Christ has suffered by it, and he might deliver us from the power of it.
5. *Remember* that those who are now in hell fire went thither for that they loved iniquity, and would not depart from it.
6. *Remember* that a profession is not worth a pin if they that make it do not depart from iniquity.
7. *Remember* that thy death-bed will be very uneasy to thee, if thy conscience at that day shall be clogged with the guilt of thy iniquity.
8. *Remember* that at the judgement-day Christ will say to those, "Depart from me," that have not here departed from their sin and iniquity.

Lastly, *Remember* well, and think much upon, what a blessed reward the Son of God will give unto them at that day that have joined to their profession of faith in him a holy and blessed conversation.[17]

Bunyan did not believe that man by himself could pursue holiness without divine assistance. He went on to encourage his readers to seek the aid of the Holy Spirit for the enabling four graces: faith, repentance, love and hope. Love to Bunyan is preeminently practical and finds its antecedent in obedience. He says, "A man cannot love God that loves not holiness; he loves not holiness that loves not God's word; he loves not God's word that does not do it."[18] In his pursuit of holiness Bunyan was no mere legalist but leaned heavy and hard upon God's grace:

---

17 *The Works of John Bunyan*, 2:518.
18 *The Works of John Bunyan*, 2:520.

Get more grace, for the more grace thou has the further is thine heart set off of iniquity, the more, also, set against it, and the better able to depart from it when it cometh to thee, and entreats thee for entertainment. Now, the way to have more grace is to have more knowledge of Christ, and to pray more fervently in his name; also, to subject thy soul and thy lusts, with all thy power, to the authority of that grace thou hast and to judge and condemn thyself most heartily before God, for every secret inclination that thou findest in the flesh to sinward.[19]

Bunyan took seriously the lifelong struggle against sin and the pursuit of holiness. He was accustomed to godly introspection, which then led to heartfelt confession and the enabling of the Holy Spirit for victory in daily life.

Ministerial success demands personal spirituality

Bunyan's writings reveal his personal conviction that ministerial spirituality is absolutely essential for ministerial faithfulness. Bunyan dearly held to the idea of a converted and called minister. He tenaciously upheld ministerial integrity, ministerial prayerfulness, ministerial faithfulness, ministerial spirituality and ministerial graciousness. Bunyan also believed in sternly warning false shepherds.

1. A converted minister

Bunyan firmly believed in a converted minister rather than a titled one. He plainly warned preachers and defenders of the gospel to ensure they were truly converted.[20] This is seen in a book written by John Bunyan in the early years of his ministry entitled *A Few Sighs from Hell*. It is based on an exposition of Luke 16:19–31. The book was first published in 1658 and went through nine publications during Bunyan's lifetime. The first publication has a rare preface from John Gifford, Bunyan's pastor at Bedford. Bunyan cautions ministers of the gospel to make sure they are soundly converted. He writes,

---

19 *The Works of John Bunyan*, 2:546.
20 *The Works of John Bunyan*, 3:723.

> Take heed that ye content not yourself with a bare notion of the Scriptures in your heads, by which you may go far, even so far as to be able to dispute for the truth, to preach the gospel, and labour to vindicate it in opposition to gainsayers, and yet be found at the left hand of Christ at the judgement-day, forasmuch as thou didst content thyself with a notion or traditional knowledge of them.

George Offor, Bunyan's editor, adds in the footnotes, "Of all men most miserable must be those clergymen and religious teachers, who, in the great day, will say, 'Lord, Lord, have we not prophesied in thy name' to whom the Lord will profess, 'I never knew you, depart, ye cursed.'"[21]

To Bunyan conversion was not merely intellectual assent to a set of biblical truths or some spiritual or emotional experience, but rather a transformed life lived under the lordship of Christ. He concludes his discourse:

> But that thou mightest be sure to escape these dangerous rocks on the right hand and on the left, see that thy faith be such as is spoken of in Scripture. And that thou be not satisfied without that, which is a faith wrought by the mighty operation of God, revealing Christ to and in thee, as having wholly freed thee from thy sins by his most precious blood. Which faith, if thou attain unto, will so work in thy heart, that first thou will see the nature of the law, and [secondly] also the nature of the gospel, and delight in the glory of it; and also thou wilt find an engaging of thy heart and soul to Jesus Christ, even to the giving up of the whole man unto him, to be ruled and governed by him to his glory, and thy comfort, by the faith of the same Lord Jesus.[22]

2. A called minister

Historically, Dissenting ministers strongly believed that the office of pastor was a sacred office to which almighty God calls and appoints his choice servants. Offor gives insight into the calling of Dissenting ministers in the time of John Bunyan:

---

21 Referring to Matthew 7:22–23.
22 *A Few Sighs from Hell, The Works of John Bunyan*, 3:724.

First, their gifts in prayer and conversation upon Divine things, and aptness in illustrating and confirming what they advance from the Scriptures, is noticed; and, secondly, they are encouraged to pray with and address the poor children in a Sunday School. If they manifest an aptness to teach, they are, thirdly, invited to give an exhortation to the church privately; and then, fourthly, they are encouraged to pray and preach among the poor in country villages and in work-houses. The God who gave the wish and the talent soon opens a way to still more public usefulness. In most cases they enter upon a course of study, to fit them for their momentous labours; but many of our most valuable ministers have, like Bunyan, relied entirely upon their prayerful investigation of the Scriptures. His college was a dungeon, his library the Bible; and he came forth with gigantic power to grapple with the prince of darkness. No human learning could have so fitted him for this terrible and mysterious warfare.[23]

Bunyan comments upon his experiences and thereby endorses the fact that every minister of the gospel must be called and set apart by God for this great and glorious office. Bunyan writes:

For after I had been about five or six years awakened, and helped myself to see both the want and worth of Jesus Christ our Lord, and also enabled to venture my soul upon him, some of the most able among the saints with us, I say the most able to judgement and holiness of life, as they conceived, did perceive that God had counted me worthy to understand something of his will in his holy and blessed Word, and had given me utterance, in some measure, to express what I saw to others for edification; therefore they desire me, and that with much earnestness, that I would be willing, at sometimes, to take in hand, in one of the meetings, to speak a word of exhortation to them.... Wherefore, to be brief, at last, being still desired by the church, after some solemn prayer to the Lord, with fasting I was more particular called forth, and appointed to a more ordinary and public preaching of the word,

---

23 *The Works of John Bunyan*, 2:41.

not only to, and amongst them that believed, but also to offer the gospel to those who had not yet received the faith thereof.[24]

3. Ministerial integrity

Bunyan was unshakably convinced that personal integrity and inner spirituality are essential for the faithful minister, since the minister is the pillar of the church and, therefore, must set forth a godly example in life and conduct. In *Solomon's Temple Spiritualized* (1688; based on Ezekiel 43:10–11), Bunyan seeks to present to his readers the wonder of the "gospel glory" of Solomon's temple. He sternly warns ministers concerning covetousness:

> Covetousness makes a minister smell frowish [disgusting odour], and look more like a greedy dog, than an apostle of Jesus Christ… they are now the pillars of the church, and they stand before the porch of the house…that the church may learn of them to be without carefulness as to worldly things, and also to be rich in love and charity towards the brethren. A covetous minister is a base thing…since all the eyes of all in the porch are upon them, be patterns and examples of good works…. O churches, let your ministers be beautified with your love, that they may beautify you with their love; and also be an ornament unto you, and to that Gospel they minister to you, for Jesus Christ's sake.[25]

4. Ministerial prayerfulness

Expounding on Christ's love, Bunyan expects every minister to sincerely love the flock committed to his care. This love is to be demonstrated through sincere and earnest prayer for the flock:

> And this in the first place, shews us the love of the minister of Jesus Christ. A minister's love to his flock is seen in his praying for them; wherefore, Paul commonly, by his epistles, either first or last, or both, gives the churches to understand, that he did often heartily pray to God for them…. And not only so, but also

---

24 *Grace Abounding to the Chief of Sinners, The Works of John Bunyan,* 1:41.
25 *Solomon's Temple Spiritualized, The Works of John Bunyan,* 3:473–475.

specifies the mercies, and blessings, and benefits which he earnestly begged for them of God.[26]

5. Ministerial faithfulness
A manuscript written and prepared by Bunyan for publication called "Paul's Departure and Crown" was one of ten found after Bunyan died. According to Offor, this manuscript bears the marks of having been composed, and perhaps preached, towards the end of Bunyan's earthly pilgrimage. In this manuscript, Bunyan expounds on 2 Timothy 4:6–8, stressing the need for faithfulness in handling the Word of God:

> This evil is to be prevented:— By a diligent watchfulness in ministers;—By a diligent preaching the word of the Lord;—and, By sound and close rebukes, reproofs, and exhortations to those in whosoever the least there appears any swerving or turning aside from the gospel. The ministers of the gospel have each of them all that authority that belongs to their calling and office, and need not to stay for power from men to put the laws of Christ in his church into due and full execution.[27]

Further on in the manuscript, Bunyan makes a number of points concerning the faithfulness of a minister of the gospel.

> *First.* If thou wouldst be faithful to do that work that God hath allotted thee to do in this world for his name, labour to live much in the favour and sense of they freedom and liberty by Jesus Christ…. *Second…*labour to see a beauty and glory in holiness, and in every good work: this tends much to the engaging of thy heart…. *Third…*make much of a trembling heart and conscience. …*Fourth…*let religion be the only business to take up thy thoughts and time…. *Fifth…*beware thou do not stop and stick when hard work comes before thee…. *Sixth…*labour away to possess thy heart with a right understanding, both of the things that this world yieldeth, and of the things that shall be hereafter….

---

26 *The Saints' Knowledge of Christ's Love, The Works of John Bunyan*, 2:12.
27 "Paul's Departure and Crown," *The Works of John Bunyan*, 1:722–723.

Seventh...beware that thou slip not, or let pass by, the present opportunity that providence layeth before thee.... *Eighth*... believe then, that whatever good thing thou dost for him, if done according to the Word, it is not only accepted by him now, but recorded, to be remembered for thee, against the time to come; yea, laid up for thee as treasure in chests and coffers, to be brought out to be rewarded before both men and angels, to thy eternal comfort, by Jesus Christ our Lord.[28]

6. Ministerial spirituality

Bunyan continues in the same discourse to write about ministerial spirituality. He expounds point four with a number of sub-points, designed to demonstrate the practical cultivation of holiness in the heart:

1. Daily bring thy heart and the Word of God together, that thy heart be levelled by it, and also filled with it....
2. A continual remembrance that to every day thou hast thy work allotted thee; and that sufficient for that day are the evils that attend thee....
3. Let thy heart be more affected with what concerns the honour of God, and the profit and glory of the gospel, than with what are thy concernments as a man, with all earthly advantages....
4. Reckon with thy own heart every day, before thou lie down to sleep, and cast up both what thou hast received from God, done for him, and where thou hast also been wanting. This will beget praise and humility, and put thee upon redeeming the day that has past...[29]

Expounding on 1 Timothy 3, Bunyan focuses on the office of the pastor and emphasizes the demands and expectations of personal spirituality in the home. He highlights four essentials of personal spirituality. One, a pastor must have a sound understanding of biblical truth and exercise biblical headship in his family (Titus 1:9; Ephesians

---

28 "Paul's Departure and Crown," *The Works of John Bunyan*, 1:731–737.
29 "Paul's Departure and Crown," *The Works of John Bunyan*, 1:733.

6:1–4). Two, a pastor should be gifted to teach, to reprove and to exhort, as should the head of the family (1 Timothy 3:2; Deuteronomy 6:7). Three, a pastor must himself be exemplary in faith and holiness, and so should the head of the family (1 Timothy 3:2–4; 4:12). Four, the pastor is to exercise leadership in getting the church together for prayer and for preaching, as indeed should the head of every household.[30]

7. *Ministerial graciousness*

Bunyan would have much to say regarding the harshness of ministers today and the hardness of their message. Bunyan rightly believed in speaking *from the heart to the heart* rather than clubbing the congregation Sunday by Sunday. Expounding on the need for ministers to act and speak graciously, he says to ministers:

> There is an incident (the direction with which one body strikes another – Ed.) in us, I know not how it doth come about, when we are converted, to contemn them that are left behind. Poor fools as we are, we forget that we ourselves were so.
>
> But would it not become us better, since we have tasted that the Lord is gracious, to carry it towards them so, that we may give them convincing ground to believe that we have found that mercy which also sets open the door for them to come and partake with us. Ministers, I say, should do thus, both by their doctrine, and in all other respects. Austerity doth not become us, neither in doctrine nor in conversation. We ourselves live by grace; let us give as we receive, and labour to persuade our fellow-sinners, which God has left behind us, to follow after, that they may partake with us of grace. We are saved by grace; let us live like those that are gracious. Let all our things, to the world, be done in charity towards them; pity them, pray for them, be familiar with them, for their grandeur; let us not walk the streets, and have such behaviours as signify we are scarce for touching of the poor ones that are left behind; no, not with a pair of tongs. It becomes not ministers thus to do.[31]

---

30 "Christian Behaviour," *The Works of John Bunyan*, 2:556.
31 "The Jerusalem Sinner Saved," *The Works of John Bunyan*, 1:98.

8. Warning against false shepherds

Bunyan sternly warns against false shepherds. He lists six marks that identify false shepherds and one to identify the true shepherd:

> Then this should teach people to be very careful, unto whom they commit the teaching and guidance of their souls. There are several sorts of shepherds in the world:
>
> 1. There are idol [*sic*. idle] shepherds (Zechariah 11:5).
> 2. There are foolish shepherds (Zechariah 11:15).
> 3. There are shepherds that feed themselves, and not their flock (Ezekiel 34:2).
> 4. There are hard-hearted and pitiless shepherds (Zechariah 11:5).
> 5. There are shepherds that, instead of healing, smite, push, and wound the diseased (Ezekiel 34:4,21).
> 6. There are shepherds that "cause their flocks to go astray" (Jeremiah 50:6).
> 7. And there are shepherds that feed their flock; these are the shepherds to whom thou shouldst commit thy soul for teaching and for guidance.[32]

Without any doubt, Bunyan's conviction that ministerial success finds its antecedent in ministerial spirituality is undeniably established.

Conclusion

John Bunyan died in 1688. His lifelong pursuit of holiness engaged his entire being. His preaching and writings reflect this ongoing passion, and his heart for personal spirituality is summed up in his "Dying Sayings" on sin: "Sin turns all God's grace into wantonness; it is the dare of his justice, the rape of his mercy, the jeer of his patience, the slight of his power, and the contempt of his love."[33]

Personal spirituality for Bunyan was a prerequisite for ministerial faithfulness and success. This passion ingrained itself on the mind and

---

32 "The Greatness of the Soul and Unspeakableness of the Loss Thereof," *The Works of John Bunyan*, 1:143.

33 "Dying Sayings," *The Works of John Bunyan*, 1:65.

heart of C.H. Spurgeon who, as we will see in the following chapter, perused Bunyan's writings as a youth and continued to walk in their path throughout his entire life and ministry.

3

Bunyan's influence on the life and ministry of Spurgeon

Spurgeon's admiration of John Bunyan

C.H. Spurgeon's admiration of John Bunyan knew no bounds. As a young man, Spurgeon engraved Bunyan's vivid characters and images, from the pages of *Pilgrim's Progress*, upon his mind and stamped them onto his gregarious heart. Bunyan's characters permeated Spurgeon's life and thought. They were used widely for illustration in his sermons, and on a personal level delighted his soul. Spurgeon's special love of *Pilgrim's Progress* is manifest in that he wrote a commentary on Bunyan's famed book entitled, *Pictures from Pilgrim's Progress*. It consists of 237 pages. He enthusiastically begins the book with, "Next to the Bible, the book that I value most is John Bunyan's *Pilgrim Progress*." Spurgeon energetically points out, "I believe I have read it through [*Pilgrim's Progress*] at least a hundred times. It is a volume of which I never seem to tire; and the secret of its freshness is that it is so largely compiled from the Scriptures."[1]

---

1   C.H. Spurgeon, *Pictures from Pilgrim's Progress* (London: Fleming H. Revell Company, 1903), 11.

Bunyan's influence on Spurgeon

Spurgeon's love for John Bunyan and his writings permeated his life. For example, John Bunyan is cited twelve times in C.H. Spurgeon's autobiographical *The Early Years*[2] and nine times in the second part of his autobiography, *The Full Harvest*.[3]

As a child, Spurgeon became acquainted with Puritan works while staying with his grandfather. It was here that the young boy was introduced to one who would become his lifelong friend, John Bunyan, through the reading of *Pilgrim's Progress*. Spurgeon writes, "Here I first struck up acquaintance with the martyrs, and especially with 'Old Bonner'[4] who burned them; next with John Bunyan and his 'Pilgrim.'"[5] He enjoyed John Bunyan so much that at an early age he committed large portions of Bunyan's writings to memory. This was apparent when, as a young man of fifteen, Spurgeon assisted J.D. Everett, another teenager in a school where Spurgeon was serving as an articled pupil. Everett—later Professor J.D. Everett, F.R.S. of Queen's College, Belfast—was very impressed with Spurgeon's memory and writes in *The Christian World* after Spurgeon's death, "I heard him recite long passages from Bunyan's *Grace Abounding*".[6]

Spurgeon's own heart and soul are interwoven with Bunyan's. This kindred spirit can be seen when Spurgeon writes, many years later:

> Oh, that you and I might get into the very heart of the Word of God, and get that Word into ourselves! As I have seen the silkworm eat into the leaf, and consume it, so aught we to do with the Word of the Lord; —not crawl over its surface, but eat right into it till we have taken it into our inmost parts. It is idle merely to let the eye glance over the words, or to recollect the poetical expressions, or the historical facts; but it is blessed to eat into the very soul of the Bible until, at last, you come to talk in Scrip-

---

2   *C.H. Spurgeon Autobiography: The Early Years, 1834–1859* (Edinburgh: The Banner of Truth Trust, 1962), 40, 65, 85, 89, 151, 164, 190, 202, 203, 223, 317, 384.

3   *C.H. Spurgeon Autobiography: The Full Harvest, 1860–1892* (Edinburgh: The Banner of Truth Trust, 1976), 26, 45, 66, 127, 156, 158, 159, 338, 386.

4   Edmund Bonner (c.1500–1569), Bishop of London.

5   *The Early Years*, 11.

6   *The Early Years*, 40.

tural language, and your very style is fashioned upon Scriptural models, and, what is better still, your spirit is flavoured with the words of the Lord. I would quote John Bunyan as an instance of what I mean. Read anything of his, and you will see that it is almost like reading the Bible itself. He has studied our Authorized Version, which will never be bettered, as I judge, till Christ shall come; he has read it till his whole being was saturated with Scripture; and, though his writings are characteristically full of poetry, yet he cannot give us his *Pilgrim's Progress*—that sweetest of all prose poems—without continually making us feel and say, "Why, this man is a living Bible!" Prick him anywhere; and you will find that his blood is Bibline, the very essence of the Bible flows from him. He cannot speak without quoting a text, for his soul is full of the Word of God.[7]

Bunyan's influence on Spurgeon's preaching
Spurgeon's lifelong perusal of the works of John Bunyan is especially obvious in his pulpit ministry. His sermons overflowed with quotations, illustrations and analogies drawn from Bunyan's writings. Investigation reveals that there are but few volumes of sermons that are absent from Bunyan's influence.[8]

An early illustration of Spurgeon citing Bunyan comes when he was twenty-five years old. On November 6, 1859, he preached to an estimated crowd of 10,000 at the Surrey Gardens Music Hall.[9] His sermon was entitled, "But It Is Good for Me to Draw Near to God" (Psalm 73:28). Pointing out the veracity of life-changing truth when learned directly from God, Spurgeon cites John Bunyan as an example:

John Bunyan says that he never forgot the divinity he taught, because it was burnt into him when he was on his knees. That is the way to learn the gospel. If you learnt it upon your knees you

---

7   *The Full Harvest*, 158–159.

8   Bunyan material can be found in *Metropolitan Tabernacle Pulpit*, vols. 1, 2, 3, 4, 8, 9, 10, 11, 12, 13, 15, 17, 20, 26, 42, 45, 46, 47, 50, 52, 53, 54, 56, 57 and 62.

9   Jesse Page, *C.H. Spurgeon His Life and Ministry* (London: Partridge and Co., 1892), 71.

will never unlearn it. That which men teach you, men can unteach you. If I am merely convinced by reason, a better reasoner may deceive me. If I merely hold my doctrinal opinions because they seem to me to be correct, I may be led to think differently another day. But if God has taught them to me—he who is himself pure truth—I have not learned amiss, but I have so learned that I shall never unlearn, nor shall I forget.[10]

At the Metropolitan Tabernacle on a Sunday morning some years later, January 15, 1865, Spurgeon refered to *Pilgrim's Progress* in an address entitled, "Knowledge Commended." Based on Daniel 11:32–33, it illustrates the need for systematic Bible reading. Spurgeon declared:

> Read the Bible consecutively: do not merely read a verse here and there—that is not fair. You would never know anything about John Bunyan's *Pilgrim's Progress* if you opened it every morning and read six lines in any part and then shut it up again; you must read it all through if you want to know anything about it.

Bunyan's influence on the Pastors' College

C.H. Spurgeon saw the Pastors' College he founded as a crucial ministry. For instance, in an address simply entitled, "Faith," delivered to a conference of ministers and the Pastors' College students on April 16, 1872, Spurgeon cited *Pilgrim's Progress* to illustrate and impress upon his hearers the absolute necessity of steadfast faith in the face of numerous enemies and obstacles. He unequivocally declared:

> I pray the Lord to endow this College with Faith. May we be an endowed and established church—established on a rock, and endowed with the blessings of the covenant of grace. Remember, brethren, that you and I are committed to faith now. It is too late to retire. We are in the condition of Bunyan's Pilgrim: we must go forward. There are many perils before us, the valley of the shadow of death lies on ahead; arrows will fly very thickly around us as we traverse its shades. 'Tis hard going on, but we cannot

---

10 *The Early Years*, 320–327.

retrace our steps, for we have no armour for our backs. Suppose we should take to reasoning, suppose we should give up the fundamentals of our faith, what would remain, to us?[11]

In *Lectures To My Students*, lecture four entitled "Books on Fables, Emblems and Parables," Spurgeon cites Bunyan and quotes extensively from his writings in the hearing of the College students:

Now, coming to parables proper, the best thing I can do for you, brethren, is to indicate where you will find some of them. And, first there is a large number, as you all know, in John Bunyan's Pilgrim's Progress. Those scenes which Christian beheld in the house of the Interpreter and in the palace called Beautiful, are some of the richest and best parables that are to be found in human literature. Indeed, with the exception of those by our Lord himself, there are none that can excel them. There is the parable of the man sweeping the room, and almost choking the pilgrim with the dust until the water was sprinkled by the damsel standing by. Then there are the two children, Passion and Patience; the fire burning against a wall, yet not quenched by water, because the flame was secretly fed by oil; the man in an iron cage; and others that I will not now call to your remembrance, but which you ought all to know by heart.[12]

Spurgeon went on to commend Bunyan's little-known book to children, with which he was well acquainted. He quotes from the book and includes Bunyan's poetry:

You may not, however, all be aware that John Bunyan wrote *A Book for Boys and Girls, Divine Emblems, or Temporal Things Spiritualized*, in which there are some excellent parables. They are really emblems; you will find them in Offor's splendid edition of

---

11 C.H. Spurgeon, *An All-Round Ministry* (Edinburgh: The Banner of Truth Trust, 1978), 30.

12 C.H. Spurgeon, *Lectures To My Students*, 4 vols. (1875–1905; reprint, Grand Rapids: Baker Books, 1980), 3:120–121.

Bunyan's works, the three volumes that you all ought to get if you can. I will not say that the poetry in these emblems excels Milton's, or even rivals Cowper's, but the sense is good. Take this one, for instance,—

"This flint, time out of mind has there abode,
Where crystal streams make their continual road;
Yet it abides a flint as much as 'twere,
Before it touched the water, or came there.

Its hardness is not in the least abated,
'Tis not at all by water penetrated.
Though water hath a soft'ning virtue in 't,
It can't dissolve the stone, for 'tis a flint.

Yea, though in water it doth still remain,
Its fiery nature still it does retain.
If you oppose it with its opposite,
Then in your very face its fire 'twill spit.

COMPARISON.
This flint an emblem is of those that lie,
Under the Word, like stones, until they die.
Its crystal streams have not their natures changed,
They are not from their lusts by grace estranged."[13]

Say what you like about the rhyme, the metaphor is a very good one.

Bunyan's influence in The Sword and the Trowel

The Sword and the Trowel, Spurgeon's monthly magazine, finds Bunyan all but omnipresent (see vols. 1, 3, 4, 5, 6). Bunyan is found in quotation, allusion or numerous earthy illustrations. As an example, in the article, "By Grace Are You Saved" in the first volume of the magazine (February 1865), we see Spurgeon pleading with sinners to repent. Using John Bunyan's narrow escapes with death as a poignant illustra-

---

13 Spurgeon, *Lectures To My Students*, 3:121.

tion of the urgency of accepting Christ, Spurgeon writes:

It is by the grace of God that ungodly men are preserved from instant death. The sharp axe of justice would soon fell the barren tree if the interceding voice of Jesus did not cry, "Spare him yet a little." Many sinners, when converted to God, have gratefully acknowledged that it was of the Lord's mercy that they were not consumed. John Bunyan had three memorable escapes before his conversion, and mentions them in his "Grace Abounding" as illustrious instances of long-suffering mercy. Occasionally such deliverances are made the means of affecting the heart with tender emotions of love to God, and grief for having offended him. Should it not be so? Ought we not to account that the long-suffering of God is salvation? (2 Peter 3:15) An officer during a battle was struck by a nearly spent ball near his waistcoat pocket, but he remained uninjured, for a piece of silver stopped the progress of the deadly missile. The coin was marked at the words DEI GRATIA *(by the grace of God)*. This providential circumstance deeply impressed his mind, and led him to read a tract which a godly sister had given him when leaving home. God blessed the reading of the tract; and he became, through the rich Face of God, a believer in the Lord Jesus. Reader, are you unsaved? Have you experienced any noteworthy deliverances? Then adore and admire the free grace of God, and pray that it may lead you to repentance![14]

When Spurgeon was sadly unable to fully celebrate his fiftieth year due to illness and forced retirement to Menton, France for rest and recovery, he prepared a leading article for *The Sword and the Trowel* called, "In my Fiftieth Year, and Getting Old." Spurgeon was going through a dry period, no doubt aggravated by illness and ongoing ministerial pressure. His struggle in sermon preparation is illustrated by a reference to Bunyan's *Pilgrim's Progress:*

---

14 C.H. Spurgeon, "By Grace Are You Saved," *The Sword and the Trowel*, February 1865 (reprint; Albany: AGES Software, 2000), 30–31.

This fiftieth year of mine has not been without its peculiar heart-searchings. When feeling weary with an unbroken stretch of work, I began to fear that it was the age of the man, as well as the work of the office, which was causing *sluggishness* of mind. We all remember how Bunyan says of his *Pilgrim's Progress*, "As I pulled it came." So did my sermons; but they wanted more pulling, and yet more.[15]

Interestingly, while steadfastly defending the faith against the inroads of Liberalism and doctrinal compromise, Spurgeon in *The Sword and the Trowel* writings known as the "Down-Grade Controversy" actually has to defend himself from his accusers who indict him with departing from the Baptist heritage. His enemies had the audacity to cite John Bunyan against him! Spurgeon swiftly and decisively responded in the December 1888 issue of *The Sword and the Trowel* in an article called "Attempts at the Impossible":

As John Bunyan has, by a thousand-horse power engine, been dragged into the Down-Grade controversy, as though he was, or would have been, opposed to our protest, we thought we would look into his works, to see if he had ever been opposed to a creed; and, as our readers will have guessed, we soon found that he had one of his own, exceedingly full and clear. It seems like a joke, that the most reckless of our opponents should attempt to put Honest John on the wrong side; and, in no spirit of jest, but in downright earnest, we suggest to any who are inclined to repeat the clumsy experiment, that they should first study Bunyan's own Confession of Faith. As we are half afraid that they will decline the task, we make them a present of his belief upon the Doctrine of Election. If they should not take delight in reading it, there may be others who will. At any rate, the Scriptural teaching which he sets forth in his homely way deserves consideration. Thus wrote the author of *The Pilgrim's Progress*.[16]

---

15 *The Full Harvest*, 386.

16 C.H. Spurgeon, "Attempts at the Impossible," *The Sword and the Trowel*, December 1888 (reprint; Albany: AGES Software, 2000), 95.

Even after Spurgeon's death, Bunyan was taken to the ends of the earth through Spurgeon's sermons published in *The Sword and the Trowel*. An excellent example is a sermon published March 5, 1908, sixteen years after Spurgeon's death (January 31, 1892) entitled "Here Am I" (1 Samuel 3:4):

> John Bunyan speaks of Eargate being stopped up with filth, and it often is so. Men cannot hear the voice of God because there is sin in the way, some darling sin; and they are not wise enough to realize that what they hear will be the means either of saving them or of damning them. Hearing true gospel sermons is one of the most solemn occupations in which intelligent beings can be employed. Hearing ears are by no means common things; happy are ye who have them.[17]

And again, published in *The Sword and the Trowel* on February 22, 1912, twenty years after Spurgeon's death, there is this extract from a sermon entitled "God's Hand at Eventide," based on Ezekiel 33:22:

> "At evening time it shall be light." In some parts of the world there is no twilight; as soon as the sun sets, night follows immediately; but here in England our long evenings are a great delight, and certainly so also is the fading evening of a well spent life, when you have to a great extent finished with the toil and turmoil of earthly service, and your soul has a blessed season of resting, as Bunyan's pilgrims had, in the land Beulah, until the summons came for them to cross the river, and go in to the presence of the king. It will be a blessed thing, to feel the hand of the lord upon us in that evening; and whether it be long or short, all will be well with all who are trusting in the Lord Jesus Christ.[18]

---

17 C.H. Spurgeon, "Here Am I," *The Sword and the Trowel*, January 31, 1892 (reprint; Albany: AGES Software, 2000), 54:145.

18 C.H. Spurgeon, "God's Hand at Eventide," *The Sword and the Trowel*, February 22, 1912 (reprint; Albany: AGES Software, 2000), 58:77.

Bunyan and Spurgeon linked in the newspapers

Even in the newspapers, Spurgeon's identification with Bunyan was established early in his ministry. When Spurgeon rocketed to fame as a young gospel preacher, his energetic preaching style and his passionate prayers were roundly criticized. A cruel and critical letter appeared in *The Essex Standard* on April 18, 1855, addressed to the editor under the signature of "A Lover of Propriety." The letter complained bitterly about Spurgeon's "profane" prayer and "prostitution of the pulpit."[19] The following week, a letter of quite another kind was published:

> Sir,—Your readers have had the opinions of two supporters of the Established Church on the preaching of the Rev. C.H. Spurgeon; and I trust to your well-known fairness to allow a Dissenter an opportunity of expressing the sentiments held by many who have enjoyed the pleasure of listening to the fervid words of that distinguished minister of the gospel.
>
> Mr. Spurgeon institutes a new era, or more correctly, revives the good old style of Bunyan, Wesley, and Whitefield—men whose burning eloquence carried conviction to the hearts of their hearers—men who cared nought for the applause of their fellow-mortals, but did all for God's glory. In the steps of these apostles does Mr. S. follow, and who could desire more noble leaders?
> — Your obedient servant, Vox Populi.[20]

Bunyan's influence on Spurgeon is life-long

In 1862, Spurgeon attended a ceremony to honour the memory of John Bunyan. Eric Hayden points out:

> In the Spring of the year [1862] there were two important and interesting incidents. John Bunyan's tomb in Bunhill Fields[21] was restored, and Spurgeon attended the ceremony with the Earl of Shaftesbury. Spurgeon spoke of Bunyan as preacher, author and

---

19 *The Early Years*, 316–317.

20 *The Early Years*, 317–318.

21 A cemetery in north London where many Nonconformist or Dissenting ministers are buried.

sufferer. He stated that he valued *The Holy War* more than *The Pilgrim's Progress*.[22]

Thirty years later, just weeks before Spurgeon died, he shared with some close friends on New Year's Eve and the following morning. The two addresses came under the title "Breaking the Long Silence,"[23] and were printed posthumously in *The Sword and the Trowel* in February 1892. In his final hours, Spurgeon once again found *Pilgrim's Progress* to be a vehicle of expression and illustration as he identifies with the writings of his lifelong friend John Bunyan:

DEAR FRIENDS, — I am not able to say much to you at present. I should have gladly invited you to prayer every morning if I had been able to meet you; but I had not sufficient strength. I cannot refrain from saying a little to you, on this the last evening of the year, by way of Retrospect, and perhaps on New Year's morning I may add a word by way of Prospect. We have come so far on the journey of life; and, standing at the boundary of another year, we look back. Let each one gaze upon his own trodden pathway. You will not need me to attempt fine words or phrases: each one, with his own eyes, will now survey his own road. Among the striking things to be noted are the dangers we have escaped. After Bunyan's Pilgrim had safely traversed the Valley of the Shadow of Death, the morning light dawned upon him, and sitting down, he looked back upon the terrible road which he had passed. It had once seemed an awful thing to him that he had marched through that valley by night; but when he looked back, and saw the horrors he had escaped, he must have felt glad that darkness had concealed much of its peril when he was actually in the midst of it. Much the same has it been with us: thank God, now that we clearly see the perils, we have passed them in safety.[24]

---

22 Eric W. Hayden, *Highlights in the Life of Charles Haddon Spurgeon* (reprint; Albany: AGES Software, 2000), 19.

23 *The Full Harvest*, 503.

24 C.H. Spurgeon, "Breaking the Long Silence," *The Sword and the Trowel*, February 1892 (reprint; Albany: AGES Software, 2000), 281.

4

John Gill's life, ministry and spirituality

The influence of John Gill

This sketch of the life and ministry of John Gill (1697–1771) reveals that the theologian-preacher of London had a substantive and lifelong influence on the life, thought and ministry of C.H. Spurgeon. In fact, Gill's theological writings were used extensively by Spurgeon not only to train future pastors, but also to undergird and buttress Spurgeon's own theological position, especially when he was embroiled in theological controversy. With a special emphasis on Gill's writing and preaching, this sketch reveals Gill's personal pursuit of spirituality, which became a model for Spurgeon to follow, and his unshakable conviction that ministerial success finds its roots in a minister's personal spirituality.

Gill's early life

John Gill was born in 1697 in Kettering, Northamptonshire, to Edward and Elizabeth Gill, Dissenting parents. They sincerely believed that their son would "prove of eminent service in the Baptist interest".[1]

---

1   Robert Oliver, "John Gill: His Life and Ministry," in Michael A.G. Haykin, ed.,

Gill's intellectual ability earned him a place at the Kettering Grammar School. Gill soon surpassed his fellow students in the mastery of Latin and Greek, and he quickly established a reputation of being an avid book reader. However, the headmaster of the school enforced a rule that every student must learn the Catechism and attend the Anglican church services. In protest, Gill's Dissenting parents removed him from school, and thus his formal education was finished at age eleven. Nevertheless, Gill was not deterred; his studious disposition was evidenced to all when he mastered Hebrew, as well as logic, philosophy and rhetoric.[2]

William Wallis (d.1711) was the pastor of the Particular Baptist church where Gill was converted at the tender age of twelve. The sermon was based on Genesis 3:9, "And the Lord called unto Adam, and said to him, where art thou?" Gill was convicted of the sinfulness of his own soul and his great need of Christ. Concerned not to make a false profession of faith, Gill waited until he was nineteen before being baptized on December 1, 1716, by Thomas Wallis (d.1726).[3] The following Sunday Gill was received into church membership and participated at the communion table. That evening, when Gill expounded on Isaiah 53, his gifts were evident to all. After one year of training at Higham-Ferrers, approximately seven miles from Kettering, he met and married Elizabeth Negus (d.1764) in 1718. In the *Memoirs* we read, "His marriage with this excellent woman, he always considered the principal object for which God sent him to that place, for she proved herself a careful, discreet and affectionate wife; and was continued to him upwards of forty-six years."[4] Gill subsequently returned to Kettering and began ministering there. The Lord was pleased to bless his ministry through a number of conversions, in particular of some lifetime friends.

The Life and Thought of John Gill (1697–1771): A Tercentennial Appreciation (New York: Brill, 1997), 8.

2   John Gill, *Body of Divinity* (1769; reprint, Georgia: Turner Lassetter, 1957), v–vii.

3   Gill, *Body of Divinity*, vi.

4   Gill, *Body of Divinity*, vii.

Gill's call to Southwark

Benjamin Keach's (1640–1704) old church at Southwark, London issued a call to Gill. The induction service was held on March 22, 1720. However, all was not well. A church split soon followed, with Gill and the majority of the church temporarily relocating and then returning to their old church home in 1720. Later a new building would be established in Carter Lane, Southwark where Gill would minister until his death in 1771.[5]

Gill's theological writings

Gill was a prolific writer and has left Christendom with a rich heritage of theological writings and commentaries. For example, Gill wrote an *Exposition of the Song of Solomon* (1728); *Exposition of the New Testament* (1746–1748); *Exposition of the Books of the Prophets of the Old Testament* (1757–1758) and *Exposition of the Old Testament* (1748–1763). Gill addressed many theological controversies in his day, which included a *Treatise on the Doctrine of the Trinity*, a defence of the orthodox teaching of the Trinity against the inroads of Sabellianism, and *The Cause of God and Truth*, a defence of the doctrines of grace. Although Gill enjoyed close friendship with two Anglican leaders, Augustus Toplady (1740–1778) and James Harvey (1714–1758), he never compromised his Baptist convictions. His *The Dissenters' Reason for Separating from the Church of England* (1751), for example, responds to a charge brought by a Welsh Anglican that Dissenters were schismatic. Another example is Gill's rejection of infant baptism. In 1766 Gill wrote the tract "Infant Baptist a Part and Pillar of Popery" against the Anglican practice of infant baptism, which he believed undermined the true church of Christ. One noteworthy citation is Gill's view of justification:

We believe that the justification of God's elect is only by the righteousness of Christ imputed to them, without the consideration of any works of righteousness done by them and that the full and free pardon of all their sins and transgressions, past, present and

5   Robert Oliver, "John Gill," in Michael A.G. Haykin, ed., *The British Particular Baptists 1638–1910* (Springfield: Particular Baptist Press, 1998), 1:147.

to come is only by the blood of Christ according to the riches of His grace.[6]

Gill's preaching

Gill's sermons are masterful in exegesis, careful, diligent and authoritative. The bulk of his application, in typical Puritan fashion, is kept to the end of the sermon. His philosophy of preaching is set forth below:

> He ought to be careful about the manner as well as the matter of his ministry; that he speak plainly, intelligibly, and boldly, the gospel, as it ought to be spoken: Elocution which is a gift of utterance, a freedom of expression, with propriety of language, is one of the gifts fitting for public usefulness in the work of the ministry; and which may be improved by the use of proper means.[7]

Gill is often accused of hyper-Calvinism. However, Tom Nettles makes a convincing argument that this is not the case. Gill believed that in preaching the minister delivers his own soul and is motivated by desires for the salvation of his hearers. Nettles cites Gill's *Duties of a Pastor*: "The Word preached by them being, by the Grace of the Spirit, an engrafted Word, is able to save them; and the Gospel being attended with the Demonstration of the Spirit, is the Power of God unto salvation."[8]

Gill's spirituality

Gregory Willis' excellent article on the spirituality of John Gill transforms the common perception of Gill from a rather fearful stoic man, to a passionate, caring pastor. Regarding spirituality of the heart, Willis points out that Gill was convinced that a Christian's heart should overflow with ecstatic love for the Lord: "a vehement affection for God and his glory...hot, burning, flaming love".[9] Gill upheld that the beauty of

---

6   Cited Oliver, "John Gill: His Life and Ministry," 20.

7   Cited in Thomas J. Nettles, "John Gill and the Evangelical Awakening," in Haykin, ed., *The Life and Thought of John Gill*, 145–146.

8   Nettles, "John Gill and the Evangelical Awakening," 149.

9   Cited in Gregory Willis, "The Fire That Burns Within: The Spirituality of John Gill," in Haykin, ed., *The Life and Thought of John Gill*, 193–194.

John Gill
(1697–1771)

Christ remained the preeminent attraction for the believer:

> Christ's whole being was "lovely and desirable," for he possessed
> "all beauty, power, wisdom and grace…holiness here appears in
> beauty, and knowledge and wisdom in perfection…. To see Him,
> the King, in his beauty, is a ravishing sight, and which fills with
> joy unspeakable and full of Glory.[10]

Gill held that spirituality has four distinct elements. First, spirituality involved communion with Christ. This embraced loving and adoring Christ in his beauty and meditating upon Christ and his grace. Second, spirituality involved worship. This involved the externals of prayer, praise and hearing the Word and the internals of godly fear, faith, trust, love and thankfulness. Third, spirituality and doctrine were absolutely essential for spiritual growth and love to God. Finally, spirituality was intimately linked to the church. This involved the blessing of God's presence, fellowship of believers (duty and love) and the Lord's table.[11]

Gill's death

Gill died on October 14, 1771, at the age of seventy-four. The sermon text at his funeral was, "For I determined not to know any thing among you, save Jesus Christ, and him crucified" (1 Corinthians 2:2). An elegy written by John Fellows (d.1785) concludes with these lines about Gill:

> And thou, blest saint! now from our scene remov'd,
> Welcom'd by angels, and by Jesus lov'd;
> May thy fair page still in our view appear,
> And be thy name to late rememb'rance dear!
> May all the labours of thy love inspire
> The sons of grace, to catch the sacred fire!
> Oh may our souls to all thy words incline,
> And may we light our dying lamps at thine!

---

10 Willis, "The Fire That Burns Within," 194.
11 Willis, "The Fire That Burns Within," 196–203.

May we, in heart and life, with thine agree,
And learn to live, and love, and die like thee!
Thy works before us lie; may he that reads
Pursue thy steps, and emulate thy deeds![12]

Ministerial success demands personal spirituality

Gill was asked to preach at the ordination of George Braithwaite (1681–1748) on March 28, 1734. He carefully chose 1 Timothy 4:16 for his text: "Take heed unto thyself, and unto thy doctrine; for in doing this, thou shalt both save thyself, and them that hear thee." Gill titled his sermon, "The Duty of a Pastor to His People."[13] As he expounded the text, we can see how Gill related spirituality to ministerial success. Gill's stated desire is evident: "In doing this [maintaining personal spirituality] you will be most likely to be instrumental in the conversion of sinners, and edification of saints. God give success to all your ministrations."

Let us then examine Gill's sermon to see how Braithwaite, or any potential minister, according to Gill, can become a "successful" minister of the gospel, and why Gill is convinced success is directly related to personal spirituality.

First, Gill emphasized the need for a successful minister to redeem the time. For Gill, redeeming the time involved cultivating personal spirituality. He emphasized prayer, meditation and daily reading of the Scriptures. Gill affirmed:

Time is precious, and ought to be redeemed, and diligently improved, by all sorts of men; but by none more than the ministers of the gospel, who should spend it in frequent prayer, constant meditation, and in daily reading the scriptures, and the writings of good men; which are transmitted to posterity for the benefit and advantage of the churches of Christ. They should give themselves up wholly to these things, and daily, and diligently study to shew themselves approved unto God, workmen that

---

12 John Fellows, *An Elegy on the Death of the Rev. John Gill, D.D.* (London, 1771).

13 "The Duty of a Pastor to His People" in John Gill, *A Collection of Sermons and Tracts* (London: George Keith, 1773), 2:1–13.

need not be ashamed, rightly dividing the word of truth (2 Tim. 2:15).[14]

Gill further reinforced the cultivation of personal spirituality by emphasizing the control of one's temper and passions. Without such inner spirituality, the minister of the gospel can in fact injure the church of Christ:

A minister ought to take heed to his spirit, his temper, and his passions, that he is not governed by them. The preachers of the gospel are men of like passions with others: Some of Christ's disciples were very hot, fiery, and passionate.... One that has the government of his passions, and can rule his own spirit and temper, is very fit to rule in the church of God. He that is slow to anger, is better than the mighty; and he that ruleth his spirit, than he that taketh a city (Prov. 16:32). But if a man is influenced and governed by his passions, he will be led by them to take indirect and imprudent steps; and to manage affairs with partiality, to the prejudice of the church, and members of it.[15]

Gill was convinced that personal spirituality is absolutely essential to the successful minister as the minister must be an example to the church in personal holiness and charity. Note in the following quote how Gill buttressed his convictions with Scripture:

A minister ought to take heed to his life and conversation, that it be exemplary to those who are under his care. Private Christians may, and ought to be examples one to another; they should be careful to maintain (Titus 3:8) or go before each other in good works; but more especially, ministers ought to be examples to the flock. This is the advice the apostle gave Timothy; be thou an example of the believers, in word, in conversation, in charity, in spirit, in faith, in purity (1 Tim. 4:12).[16]

---

14 "The Duty of a Pastor to his People," 2:5.
15 "The Duty of a Pastor to his People," 2:6.
16 "The Duty of a Pastor to his People," 2:6.

Gill was confident that since personal spirituality is absolutely essential for gospel success, the converse was also true; namely, that an ungodly minister results in a useless and unprofitable ministry. He thus cautioned Braithwaite and others:

> They [ministers] ought to be careful how they behave themselves in their families, in the church, and in the world; that they give no offense in anything, that the ministry be not blamed, and so become useless and unprofitable. This was what the apostle Paul was careful of, with respect to himself, and his ministry; "I keep under my body, and bring it into subjection" (1 Cor. 9:27). …lest he should be guilty of misconduct in his outward conversation among men; and so become rejected, and disapproved of by men, and be useless in his ministry. The name of God, the ways of Christ, and the truths of the gospel, are blasphemed, and spoken evil of, through the scandalous lives of professors, and especially ministers. Nothing is more abominable than that one, whose business it is to instruct and reprove others, [who] is himself notoriously culpable.[17]

Gill concluded his sermon by driving home the importance of personal spirituality for ministerial success:

> And I conclude, that these will also engage you to take heed to your doctrine; that it be according to the scriptures, the doctrine of Christ, his apostles, and true godliness; and such as will be profitable to them that hear it; that it be found and incorrupt, pure and unmixed, and consistent with itself; that it be delivered out in the best manner you are able, and defended, to the utmost of your ability, by which you will abide, and in which you will continue: In doing this you will be most likely to be instrumental in the conversion of sinners, and edification of saints. God give success to all your ministrations.[18]

---

17 "The Duty of a Pastor to his People," 2:7.
18 "The Duty of a Pastor to his People," 2:13.

On September 20, 1767, Gill preached at the funeral of William Anderson (d. 1767), a friend and fellow Baptist pastor. His sermon, a detailed exposition of 2 Timothy 4:7–8, was called "The Faithful Minister of Christ Crowned." After carefully expounding the text, Gill makes a number of personal comments about William Anderson. He stressed that Anderson's ministry was successful in that he was exemplary not only in his faithful labours for Christ but also in his gracious conduct among God's people. He affirms that Anderson left a lucrative position in business to minister to a rather poor congregation, which resulted in personal economic hardship. Yet, without complaint Anderson laboured on and was ultimately blessed by God, being a witness to conversions and the edification of God's people. Gill further declared that this congregation, which was so greatly blessed, sadly rejected Anderson and left him destitute. Nevertheless, Anderson's gracious spirit was not extinguished. He pressed on despite the grief of rejection and continued to minister faithfully to a small group from the church. Here we see that godly character evidenced in faithful ministry resulted in God's blessing:

> I am persuaded, that neither the memory of any man living, nor perhaps the history of any age, can furnish an instance similar to this case; that a worthy minister of the gospel should be divested of his office, and turned out of his place, when no charge, neither of immorality nor of false doctrine, was laid against him. Such hard usage did this faithful minister of Christ meet with, these were the wounds he received in the house of those he once thought his friends; the pain of which went to his heart, and the anguish thereof drank up his spirits. Nevertheless he ceased not from his Master's work; and which he performed with more vigour, comfort and cheerfulness, than could have been expected, among those few that cleaved unto him, and abode with him.[19]

---

19 "The Faithful Minister of Christ Crowned," *A Collection of Sermons and Tracts*, 1:607.

Anderson's faithfulness, according to Gill, resulted in ministerial success. This success was evidenced in numerical growth and being the instrument for church edification. Highlighting the faithful labours of Anderson, Gill declared,

> He left a very lucrative employment to serve them, and the interest of Christ among them, on which his heart was set; and it pleased God to bless his labours, both for edification and conversion, so that there was an increase both of audience and members; and he laid himself out indefatigably to serve them, both as to their temporals and spirituals: by his means, and through his interest, a commodious house for worship was built, which they greatly wanted.[20]

Gill concluded the sermon by encouraging the little flock that was now shepherdless. In so doing, we note the interconnectedness of personal spirituality and ministerial success in the mind of Gill:

> If God should send you a pastor, to feed you with knowledge and understanding, which I perceive you have some hope of; if God should bless his labours, the place of your tent may be enlarged, and the curtains of your habitations may be stretched forth, and God may increase you with men as a flock; frequently meet together, pray earnestly and constantly, who knows but God may have a blessing in store for you? To conclude; since we have all in one shape or another a warfare to war, a race to run, and a trust to discharge; let us manfully fight till the warfare is accomplished; and run, with patience and diligence, the remainder of the race set before us; and faithfully perform the trust reposed in us; that when all is done and over, we may enjoy the crown of righteousness, which is in common provided for all that love the appearing of Christ.[21]

---

20 "The Faithful Minister of Christ Crowned," 1:606–607.
21 "The Faithful Minister of Christ Crowned," 1:608.

Conclusion

In studying Gill's scholarly writings and sermon manuscripts there is no doubt that Gill significantly contributed to the understanding of Baptist thought and polity. One cannot but thank God for this intellectual giant, who graciously yet firmly addressed the rise of heterodoxy in his generation, and generations yet unborn, through his writings. Spurgeon followed Gill in this regard, as he, like Gill, would battle for truth against many in the Down-Grade Controversy.

Gill's convergence of clear theological insight and a passionate devotion to the glory, beauty and holiness of the living God would make an ineradicable imprint on the mind and heart of C.H. Spurgeon—in particular, Gill's conviction that spirituality has a direct correlation with ministerial success.

5

Gill's influence on the life and ministry of Spurgeon

Spurgeon's admiration of John Gill

Spurgeon's lifelong admiration of Gill is made apparent in a variety of ways, from sermon quotations and illustrations, in lectures to his ministerial students, throughout his personal letters, and even in his own library.

Gill's influence in Spurgeon's sermons

Spurgeon's sermons reflect a high esteem of Gill. In the early days of Park Street Baptist Chapel to the last years of his ministry at the Metropolitan Tabernacle, Gill was cited extensively.[1]

For instance, Spurgeon cites Gill's commentary to illustrate a point in one of his earliest sermons at Park Street Baptist Chapel, "Marvellous Increase of the Church," based on Isaiah 60:8:

> But methinks there is another idea here, which Dr. Gill gives us in his very valuable commentary. "Who are these that fly as a

---

1 See, for example, *Metropolitan Tabernacle Pulpit*, vols. 1, 2, 3, 4, 7, 9, 10, 12, 14, 15, 17, 27, 31, 45, 48, 49, 50, 51, 54, 55.

cloud," for unanimity; You will mark not as clouds, but "as a cloud," not as two or three bodies, but as one united and compact mass! Here is the secret of strength. Split us into fractions and we are conquered; unite us into a steady phalanx, and we become invincible; knit us together as one man, and Satan himself can never rend us asunder. Divide us into threads, let our warp and woof be disunited, and we become like rotten tow, that burneth before a single spark of the fire of the enemy. But, thanks be to God, we are "as the heart of one man."[2]

In another sermon, this time at Exeter Hall, Spurgeon cites John Gill alongside John Calvin (1509–1564) as theological authorities, yet he argues that the Word of God must remain our ultimate authority to establish the doctrine of election, not men. In the sermon "Election and Holiness" preached on March 11, 1860, from the text Deuteronomy 10:14–16, Spurgeon declared, "The Arminian trembles to go an inch beyond Arminius or Wesley, and many a Calvinist refers to John Gill or John Calvin, as any ultimate authority."[3] In Spurgeon's latter years, while preaching the sermon "The Helmet of Hope," based on 1 Thessalonians 5:8, at the Metropolitan Tabernacle in 1866, Spurgeon cites an event in Gill's life. Gill was threatened that if he continued to proclaim certain doctrines, the person would leave the church and the church would suffer financially. He cites Gill's response, "'I can afford to be poor,' said Dr. Gill, when one of his subscribers threatened to give up his seat, and would not attend, if the doctor preached such and such a doctrine."[4]

Gill's influence in The Sword and the Trowel
In an article, "Use the Pen," in the 1871 volume of *The Sword and the Trowel*, Spurgeon writes to encourage young men to not only preach the Word, but like Gill and others take up their quills and write:

> The utterance of truth with the living voice is their main business, and for many reasons this deserves their chief attention; but the

---

2   "Marvellous Increase of the Church," *The New Park Street Pulpit*, 2:75.

3   "Election and Holiness," *The New Park Street Pulpit*, 6:133.

4   "The Helmet of Hope," *The Metropolitan Tabernacle Pulpit*, 55:509.

publishing of the same truth by means of the press is barely second in importance, and should be used to the full measure of each man's ability. …Young men, look to your goosequills, your Gillets, or your Waverleys, and see if you cannot write for Jesus.[5]

Gill's influence in Spurgeon's personal letters

Three letters of Spurgeon that explicitly cite Gill include one written in his youth to his father, one requesting his friend to secure Gill's commentaries for his son, and another written in the midst of controversy to the leaders of the Metropolitan Tabernacle.

Spurgeon wrote to his father, John Spurgeon, in early 1854 at the beginning of his ministry, "The portraits of Gill and Rippon—large as life—hang in the vestry."[6] (Both Gill and Rippon, like Spurgeon, were exceptionally young, in their early twenties, when called to the Southwark congregation). Another letter was written to his friend J.L. Keys (Spurgeon's editorial secretary, researcher and proofreader) to secure a set of Gill's commentaries and other books for his son Charles' birthday. He wrote, "I want a good and cheap copy of Gill's commentary for my son Charles…. These are for a birthday present for next Friday and must not be very shabby but of course are second-hand."[7]

While in the crucible of affliction, due to the flood of critics in the Down-Grade Controversy, Spurgeon wrote to the co-pastor and deacons of the Metropolitan Tabernacle to encourage them in the midst of the battle. In doing so, he cited John Gill as an example of steadfastness in the midst of controversy. He wrote:

Menton, France November 27, 1887.

My eminent predecessor, Dr. Gill, was told, by a certain member of his congregation who ought to have known better, that, if he published his book, *The Cause of God and Truth*, he would lose some of his best friends, and that his income would fall off. The

---

5   *The Sword and the Trowel*, 1871, 3:72.
6   *Letters of Charles Haddon Spurgeon* (Edinburgh: The Banner of Truth Trust, 1992), 47–49.
7   *Letters of Charles Haddon Spurgeon*, 88.

doctor said, "I can afford to be poor, but I cannot afford to injure my conscience;" and he has left his mantle as well as his chair in our vestry. ...Yours forever, C.H. SPURGEON.[8]

Gill's influence in the Pastors' College

Spurgeon's appreciation and admiration of John Gill is substantiated by his address to his theological students at the Pastors' College, recorded in *Commenting and Commentaries*. Spurgeon's approval of Gill as a pastor-theologian is clearly evident:

> A very distinguished place is due to DR. GILL. Beyond all controversy, Gill was one of the most able Hebraists of his day, and in other matters no mean proficient.... His great work on the Holy Scriptures is greatly prized at the present day by the best authorities, which is conclusive evidence of its value, since the set of the current of theological thought is quite contrary to that of Dr. Gill... Gill's laurels as an expositor are still green. His ultraism is discarded, but his learning is respected: the world and the church take leave to question his dogmatism, but they both bow before his erudition. Probably no man since Gill's days has at all equalled him in the matter of Rabbinical learning... Gill was a master cinder sifter among the Targums, the Talmuds, the Mishna, and the Gemara...[9]

Spurgeon's humour is apparent in the following remark about his esteem of Gill's prolific output as he shared with his students:

> He was always at work; it is difficult to say when he slept, for he wrote 10,000 folio pages of theology. The portrait of him which belongs to this church, and hangs in my private vestry, and from which all the published portraits have been engraved, represents him after an interview with an Arminian gentleman, turning up his nose in a most expressive manner, as if he could not endure

---

8 *Autobiography*, 4:261–262.

9 C.H. Spurgeon, *Commenting and Commentaries* (London, 1876; reprint, Edinburgh: The Banner of Truth Trust, 1969), 8.

even the smell of freewill. In some such a vein he wrote his commentary. He hunts Arminianism throughout the whole of it. He is far from being so interesting and readable as Matthew Henry. He delivered his comments to his people from Sabbath to Sabbath, hence their peculiar mannerism.[10]

Spurgeon valued Gill's theological insights and stated, "For good, sound, massive, sober sense in commenting, who can excel Gill?" Yet Spurgeon is not blinded by his admiration. He also warned his students,

Very seldom does he allow himself to be run away with by imagination, except now and then when he tries to open up a parable, and finds a meaning in every circumstance and minute detail; or when he falls upon a text which is not congenial with his creed, and hacks and hews terribly to bring the word of God into a more systematic shape.[11]

Commenting on Gill's commentary on the Song of Solomon, Spurgeon writes:

The best thing Gill ever did. He could not exhaust his theme, but he went as far as he could towards so doing. He is occasionally fanciful but his work is precious. Those who despise it have never read it or are incapable of elevated spiritual feelings.[12]

Gill's portrait, chair and pulpit were retained by Spurgeon; in fact the pulpit was used by the ministerial students to keep them, as Spurgeon put it, sound in their theology!

Spurgeon's appreciation of Gill's books

Spurgeon took great delight in obtaining signed photographs of authors that he particularly enjoyed. Moreover, he would record special events in his life in his more prized collection of books. Here, we see Spurgeon's

---

10 *Commenting and Commentaries*, 9.
11 *Commenting and Commentaries*, 9.
12 *Commenting and Commentaries*, 113.

high esteem of Gill. Spurgeon as a young pastor at Waterbeach began to save and acquire volumes of Gill. This continued as he continually saved his money to make monthly instalments to acquire Gill's commentaries. Moreover, we see that Spurgeon took great delight in writing in each volume some special event. This spanned his pastoral ministry from his youth in Waterbeach to his senior years at the Metropolitan Tabernacle:

> The following inscriptions, in Mr. Spurgeon's handwriting, are in his set of volumes of Dr. Gill's *Commentary*:—
>
> In Vol I. — I subscribed for this and took the monthly parts. C.H. Spurgeon, 1852
>
> To this author's pulpit I was able to succeed in 1854.
>
> C.H. Spurgeon,
Living in Cambridge,
Baptist Minister of Waterbeach
>
> In April, 1854, unanimously elected Pastor of the Same Church, which once met in Carter Lane, under Dr. Gill, and then Dr. Rippon,—now Park Street Southwark.
>
> In Vol. V.—I subscribed to these vols. of Gill in monthly parts, and had them bound. December, 1852.
>
> In Vol VI.—Many sneer at Gill, but he is not to be dispensed with. In some respects, he has no superior. He is always well worth consulting. C.H.S. 1886.[13]

To summarize, beyond any doubt, Spurgeon had a lifelong esteem of Gill's astute theological mind and, even more so, Gill's conviction that there is a clear correlation between spirituality and ministerial success.

---

13 *Autobiography*, 1:254–255.

6

Andrew Fuller's life, ministry and spirituality

The influence of Andrew Fuller

This sketch of the life and ministry of Andrew Fuller (1754–1815) introduces a man whose theological writings and personal spirituality would greatly influence the life and ministry of Charles Spurgeon, and countless Baptists to the present day. In addition to the writings of John Bunyan and John Gill, Spurgeon's convictions about ministerial spirituality also find their root in Andrew Fuller.

Fuller's early life and conversion

Andrew Fuller was born on February 6, 1754, to Robert Fuller (1723–1781) and his wife Philippa Gunton (1726–1816). Both parents were Baptists by conviction and they, in turn, had come from Dissenting families. Although Andrew Fuller was brought up in a Christian home and faithfully attended church, he did not hear a faithful articulation of the gospel since hyper-Calvinism was then in vogue. This impeded Fuller's understanding of the grace of God. He was convinced that he did not have the qualifications to merit fleeing to Christ. However, as a young man of fifteen, in 1769, he experienced conversion. Here is his description of this wonderful event:

I must—I will—yes, I will trust my soul—my sinful—lost soul in his hands. If I perish, I perish. However it was I was determined to cast myself upon Christ, thinking peradventure he would save my soul...and as the eye of the mind was more and more fixed upon him, my guilt and fears were gradually and insensibly removed.... I now found rest for my troubled soul. When I thought of the gospel way of salvation, I drank it in as cold water is imbibed by a thirsty man. My heart felt one with Christ, and dead to every other object around me...I now knew experimentally what it was to be dead to the world by the cross of Christ.[1]

Fuller was baptized the next year at Soham Baptist Church in Cambridgeshire. Although he had only received a primary school education, Fuller became very interested in the theological discussions and trends of his day. He read widely, drawing from Bunyan, the Puritan divine John Owen (sometimes called the "Calvin of England"), John Gill and Jonathan Edwards (1703–1758), probably the greatest theologian of the eighteenth century. In 1775, Andrew Fuller was ordained and served as pastor of Soham Baptist Church until 1782 when he moved to the Baptist church in Kettering.

Fuller's preaching

In reading his sermons one cannot fail to see that Andrew Fuller was a careful expositor of God's Word. He was diligent and skilful as he exegeted the text and, in a masterly fashion, inculcated life-giving truth into the minds and hearts of his hearers. For instance, he declared in his sermon "On Preaching Christ" that it is essential to preach Christ clearly and boldly, as well as to call all to live piously in the presence of Christ:

Preach Christ, or you had better be anything than a preacher. The necessity laid on Paul was not barely to preach, but to preach Christ. "Woe is me, if I preach not the gospel".... Some are

---

1   John Ryland, *The Work of Faith, the Labour of Love, and the Patience of Hope, Illustrated; in the Life and Death of the Reverend Andrew Fuller* (London: Button and Son, 1816), 20–21, 29–30.

employed in depreciating Christ. But do you honour him. Some who talk much about him, yet do not preach him, and by their habitual deportment prove themselves enemies of his cross…. If you preach Christ, you will not fear for want of matter. His person and work are rich in fullness. Every divine attribute is seen in him. All the types prefigure him. The prophecies point to him. Every truth bears relation to him. The law itself must be so explained and enforced as to lead to him.[2]

Fuller's championing of truth

Welsh author David Phillips acknowledged Fuller as the outstanding Baptist theologian of his day (the eighteenth century) by affectionately describing him as the "Elephant of Kettering."[3] Fuller was indeed a mighty champion for truth. Throughout his life, he faithfully battled against heterodoxy[4] in a bold and yet gracious manner. We can sense this passion for truth in his sermon "The Nature of the Gospel and the Manner in Which it Ought To Be Preached." Fuller declares:

He that is afraid or ashamed to preach the whole of the gospel, in all its implications and bearings, let him stand aside: he is utterly unworthy of being a soldier of Jesus Christ. Sometimes, if you would speak the whole truth, you may be reproached as unsound and heterodox. But you must not yield to popular clamour. If you have truth on your side, stand firm against all opposition.[5]

Many of Fuller's numerous writings were designed to combat heterodoxy in his day. His *magnum opus*, *The Gospel Worthy of All Acceptation* (1785), unequivocally championed the biblical truth that there is no contradiction between election and human responsibility.

A second example of such polemic writings is Fuller's treatise

2 Andrew Gunton Fuller, ed., *The Complete Works of the Rev. Andrew Fuller*, 5 vols. (London: Holdsworth and Ball, 1831), 4:481.

3 David Phillips, *Memoir of the Life, Labors, and Extensive Usefulness of the Rev. Christmas Evans* (New York: M.W. Dodd, 1843), 74.

4 Meaning that which is characterized by departure from accepted beliefs and standards; not orthodox, but not sufficiently different so as to be called heretical.

5 Fuller, *Complete Works of Andrew Fuller*, 3:470.

against Socinianism. In a series of fifteen letters, Fuller exposes the heresy and destructive nature of the leading Socinian doctrines, namely the rejection of the deity and atonement of Christ.[6]

Fuller's support of missions

Andrew Fuller's passion for souls is evidenced in his involvement in the formation of a monthly prayer meeting dedicated to seeking revival and the conversion of sinners around the world. It was from this prayer meeting that the Baptist Missionary Society was born. Fuller was its secretary from 1793 till his death in 1815. He faithfully sought to raise funds to support William Carey (1761–1834) in India, their first missionary and Andrew Fuller's close friend. Fuller was tireless in promoting the Missionary Society and travelled extensively throughout England, Scotland and Wales, and once to Ireland, seeking to raise support. Humanly speaking, without Andrew Fuller there would have been no William Carey.

Thomas J. Nettles notes:

> Andrew Fuller not only championed the cause of foreign missions, but strongly defended the Doctrines of Grace. The modern foreign-mission movement was founded upon thoroughgoing commitment to the absolute sovereignty of God, coupled with uncompromising insistence upon the full responsibility of man.[7]

Fuller's personal spirituality

Andrew Fuller sincerely strove to live a pious life. He was tenacious in his belief that it is not so much the use of talents that determines our eternal reward as much as our spirituality. Preaching on "The Christian Doctrine of Rewards" he declares, "The reward as promised in the Gospel will not be so much according to the talents we possess as the use we make of them; nor so much in respect of our success as of our fidelity."[8]

---

6   Fuller, *Complete Works of Andrew Fuller*, 2:211.

7   Thomas J. Nettles, *By His Grace and For His Glory* (Grand Rapids: Baker Book House, 1986), 129.

8   Fuller, *Complete Works of Andrew Fuller*, 4:91.

In order to understand his inner struggles to live a pious life, we turn to those entries in his diary that relate to his ministerial work. As he wrote in 1780, he yearned to be of service to God: "I longed in prayer to-night to be more useful. O that God would do somewhat by me! Nor is this, I trust, from ambition, but from a pure desire to work for God, and the benefit of my fellow-sinners."[9] Struggling with his own personal spirituality and linking it to the success of his ministry, Fuller wrote on February 4, 1781: "Some pleasure in preaching…but I fear my ministry will never be of much use. I fear a dead weight of carnal-mindedness and stupor in me will always prove an obstacle to usefulness."[10] He was ever conscious of the gravity of preaching and how it impacted his own soul. He stated:

> Feb. 5, 1781: A pulpit seems an awful place! An opportunity for addressing a company of immortals on their eternal interests—O how important! We preach for eternity. We in a sense are set for the rising and falling of many in Israel. And our own rise and fall is equally therein involved.[11]

Fuller's family

Fuller was familiar with personal trials. He married Sarah Gardiner (1756–1792) on December 23, 1776. They had eleven children, of which seven died in infancy. When Sarah also died after sixteen years of marriage, Fuller remarried two years later. His second wife, Ann Coles (1763–1825), bore six children of whom three died in infancy. Reading in his diary of how he drew comfort from God in deep and dark days is a powerful encouragement. Fuller's faith never seriously wavered, and his heart never grew angry at the providence of God, even when he sat up all night watching the last hours of his daughter Ann, his twenty-month-old baby. In the morning, his wife found a poem written by his hand glorifying his God:

---

9 Ryland, *The Work of Faith*, 131.
10 Ryland, *The Work of Faith*, 134.
11 Ryland, *The Work of Faith*, 134.

Oh our Redeemer, and our God our help
   In tribulation—hear our fervent prayer!
To THEE we now resign the sacred trust...

In THEE a refuge may she find in death,
   And in thy bosom dwell when torn from ours!
Into thy hands her spirit we commit,
   In hope 'ere long to meet and part no more.[12]

When his oldest son Robert proved unstable and drifted through life with numerous failed occupations, what was most grievous to Fuller was that he had no clear profession of faith in Christ. However, Fuller's love never waned. As a father, he pled to God for his son's soul, time after time, year after year. The young man died in March 1809 after a lingering illness.[13] Sometime afterward, Fuller received confirmation that God had answered his prayers and that his son was trusting in Christ in the last days of his life.

His second wife, Ann, wrote concerning the character of her husband: "I must testify to have been, ever since I had the happiness of being united to him, of the most amiable and endearing kind."[14] Expressing her concern over his long hours of labour, she recalls his response, "Ah, my dear, the way for us to have any joy, is to rejoice in all our labour, and then we shall have plenty of joy."[15] Fuller never wasted time or energy on the trivial. His delight was to discuss Christ or theological issues with his close friends. His wife once remarked of him, "He had a heart formed for the warmest, sincerest friendship with those whose minds were congenial with his own, and who were engaged in similar pursuits."[16]

His love for God is clearly evidenced, not only in his long multifaceted labours but even on his deathbed:

---

12 Ryland, *The Work of Faith,* 474.
13 Ryland, *The Work of Faith,* 483.
14 Ryland, *The Work of Faith,* 475.
15 Ryland, *The Work of Faith,* 475.
16 Ryland, *The Work of Faith,* 476.

Andrew Fuller
(1754–1815)

On the Lord's-day morning on which he died, May 7, 1815, he said to his daughter Sarah, "I wish I had strength enough."... She asked, "To do what?" He replied, "To worship, child."[17]

Speaking at Fuller's funeral, his confidant and friend John Ryland (1753–1825) summarized Fuller's love and devotion to God. He said:

As it was, he certainly did more for God than most good men could have effected in a life longer by twenty years. And while others admired his zeal and activity, he kept a constant watch over his own heart, and was perpetually applying to himself the Divine interrogative—*Did ye do it unto me?* None who knew him could doubt the singleness and purity of his intention.... Though conscious of integrity (of which I never saw stronger evidence of any man of my acquaintance), yet conscious also to himself of unnumbered defects, he cast himself into the arms of the omnipotent Saviour, and died, as he had long lived—*Looking for the mercy of our Lord Jesus Christ unto eternal life.*[18]

Ministerial success demands personal spirituality

As a highly respected and esteemed Baptist minister, Andrew Fuller was often called upon to preach at ordination services. It is here, more than anywhere else, that we observe Fuller's unshakable conviction that successful ministry finds its antecedent in the personal spirituality of the minister.

Particularly noteworthy is the charge he brought to Rev. Robert Fawkner at his ordination service in Thorn, Bedfordshire, on October 31, 1787. Fuller chose Acts 11:24 for his text: "He was a good man, and full of the Holy Spirit, and of faith; and much people was added to the Lord." He entitled his message "The Qualifications and Encouragement of a Faithful Minister Illustrated by the Character and Success of Barnabas."[19]

---

17 Ryland, *The Work of Faith*, 550.

18 Ryland, *The Work of Faith*, 581–582.

19 "The Qualifications and Encouragement of a Faithful Minister Illustrated by the Character and Success of Barnabas" in Fuller, *Complete Works of Andrew Fuller*,

The burden of his message is that ministerial success is directly associated with personal spirituality. Therefore, if the minister sincerely desires the blessings of the Lord upon his labours, the minister must earnestly pursue personal spirituality—even over the cultivation of spiritual gifts. Fuller expounded the text, seeking to demonstrate from the life of Barnabas and other biblical examples, as well as from church history, the maxim that success in ministry is interlinked and interwoven with ministerial spirituality. We will examine this ordination sermon at length since it is pivotal to seeing this conviction held by Fuller.

First, Fuller called upon Robert Fawkner to pursue the goodness emulated by Barnabas.

As he loved Christ, so he loved his people. He appears to have possessed much of the tender and affectionate, on account of which he was called Barnabas—a son of consolation.... If we would describe one that more than ordinarily shines in spirituality, meekness, and kindness, we know not how to speak of him better than to say, with a degree of emphasis, He is a good man. After this eminence in goodness, brother, may it be your concern, and mine, daily to aspire![20]

Fuller went on to exhort Fawkner to cultivate good character in every facet of his life:

My dear brother, value the character of a good man in All the parts of your employment; and above all, in those things which the world counts great and estimable.... Value it at home and in your family.... Value this character in your private retirements. Give yourself up to the Word of God and prayer.... Value it in your public exercises.... Value it in the general tenor of your behaviour.[21]

4:25–39.
20 Fuller, *Complete Works of Andrew Fuller*, 4:26-27.
21 Fuller, *Complete Works of Andrew Fuller*, 4:29.

Fuller maintained that without godly spirituality the message of the gospel will not bring success, even if the preacher is eminently gifted:

> Cultivate a meek, modest, peaceful and friendly temper...be pitiful, be courteous. It is this, my brother, that will recommend the gospel you proclaim. Without this, could you preach with the eloquence of an angel, you may expect that no good end will be the answer.[22]

In a world that is enthralled with gifts rather than personal spirituality, Andrew Fuller has much to say to our generation:

> If we improve in gifts and not in grace to say the least, it will be useless and perhaps dangerous both to ourselves and others. To improve in gifts, that we may be the better able to discharge our work, is laudable; but, if it be for the sake of popular applause, we may expect a blast. Hundreds of ministers have been ruined by indulging the thirst for the character of the *great* man, while they have neglected the far superior character of the *good* man.[23]

In the final point of his sermon, Fuller drove home with great passion the idea that ministry success is contingent upon personal spirituality. Expounding the phrase "and much people was added to the Lord," Fuller affirmed that the blessing of God poured out upon Barnabas was contingent upon the personal spirituality of Barnabas. He stated:

> The connection between such additions and eminence in grace and holiness in a minister, deserves our serious attention. I think it may be laid down as a rule, which both Scripture and experience will confirm, that *eminent spirituality in a minister is usually attended with eminent usefulness....* Our want of usefulness is often to be ascribed to our want of spirituality, much oftener than

---

22 Fuller, *Complete Works of Andrew Fuller*, 4:29.
23 Fuller, *Complete Works of Andrew Fuller*, 4:30.

to our want of talents. God has frequently been known to succeed men of inferior abilities, when they have been eminent for holiness, while he blasted others of much superior talents, when that quality has been wanting. Hundreds of ministers, who, on account of their gifts, have promised to be shining characters, have proved the reverse: and all owing to such things as pride, unwatchfulness, carnality, and levity.[24]

Fuller further expounded this with three sub-points in the final section of his sermon:

Eminence in grace, my brother, will contribute to your success in three ways:—
1. It will fire your soul with *holy love to Christ and the souls of men*; and as such a spirit is usually attended with success. I believe you will find that, in almost all the great works which God has wrought, in any period of time, he has honoured men of this character, by making them his instruments. 2. Eminence in grace will *direct your ends to the glory of God; and the welfare of men's souls*; and, where this is the case, it is usually attended with a blessing. 3. Eminence in grace will enable you to *bear prosperity in your ministry without being lifted up with it; and so contribute towards it.*[25]

Fuller underscored the relationship of spirituality with ministerial success by citing a number of biblical characters: Aaron, Ezra and Nehemiah. He concluded this point with a brief survey of church history:

Time would fail me to speak of all the great souls, both inspired and uninspired, whom the King of kings has delighted to honour; of Paul, and Peter, and their companions; of Wickliff [i.e. John Wycliffe], and Luther, and Calvin, and many others at the Reformation; of [John] Elliot, and Edwards, and Brainerd, and Whitefield, and hundreds more whose names are held in esteem in the

24 Fuller, *Complete Works of Andrew Fuller*, 4:36–37.
25 Fuller, *Complete Works of Andrew Fuller*, 4:37–38.

Church of God. These were men of God; men who had great grace, as well as gifts; whose hearts burned in love for Christ and the souls of men. They looked upon their hearers as their Lord had done upon Jerusalem, and wept over them. In this manner they delivered their messages; "and much people were added unto the Lord."[26]

According to Fuller, lack of spirituality is a barrier to God's blessings, since it will pervert the blessing of God into an occasion of sinful pride or selfish ambition. He sternly warns, "but if we pursue separate and selfish ends, we walk contrary to God, and may expect God to walk contrary to us."[27]

Fuller is convinced that God may not choose to bless, because we have not the grace to bear it. He says, "I am often afraid lest this should be one considerable reason why most of us have no more real success in our work than we have; perhaps it is not safe for us to be owned much of God; perhaps we have not grace enough to bear prosperity."[28]

Lack of spirituality leads to ministerial failure

As we have seen, Fuller definitely links ministerial spirituality to ministerial success. Therefore, in his mind the converse is also true: lack of spirituality results in ministerial failure. This is set forth in a sermon preached by Fuller entitled, "The Nature of the Gospel and the Manner in which it Ought to be Preached."[29] Fuller urged fellow ministers to live a pious life, or else they cannot rightly preach the gospel. He states:

> O! If we preach the gospel as we ought to preach it, what fidelity is here required! You must, my brother, side with God against an ungodly world...—you must be faithful.[30]

26 Fuller, *Complete Works of Andrew Fuller*, 4:37–38.
27 Fuller, *Complete Works of Andrew Fuller*, 4:38.
28 Fuller, *Complete Works of Andrew Fuller*, 4:38.
29 "The Nature of the Gospel and the Manner in which it Ought to be Preached" in Fuller, *Complete Works of Andrew Fuller*, 4:469–472.
30 Fuller, *Complete Works of Andrew Fuller*, 4:470.

Fuller moved on to expound this need. He pointed out that the results of a lack of spirituality will not only be failure in ministry but the most serious of consequences. He warned against lack of spirituality and sincerity when he declared:

> Consider the examples exhibited for your warning. —Some have sunk into indolence and self-indulgence; sauntering about and gossiping, instead of preaching, from house to house; and there has been an end of them. Some have risen into pride and priestly insolence, and there has been an end of them. Some have trifled with the truth, and God has given them up to destructive error. Others have plunged into political speculations, which have eaten up all their religion: aiming to govern the world, they have lost the government of their own souls, and of their peculiar charge…. My brother, be faithful, and you shall receive a crown. If you be not, the eternal curse of God awaits you![31]

Conclusion

In reading Andrew Fuller's life, sermons, diary and letters one cannot but thank God for this "Elephant of Kettering." Andrew Fuller is truly a spiritual giant who transformed lives through his preaching, who strengthened the evangelical movement through his writings and who impacted the world through his tireless support of missionary activities. Moreover, we learn from Andrew Fuller that ministerial success finds its antecedent in personal spirituality. Conversely, ministerial failure finds its antecedent in a lack of spirituality.

Andrew Fuller is a multi-faceted example: as a pastor he loved and cared for his people; as a preacher he was expositional and Christocentric; as a theologian he was orthodox, discerning, warm and practical; as a writer he was biblical, exegetical and insightful; and, as a visionary for missions, few could equal his zeal and love—a true friend and rope-holder for William Carey.

---

31 Fuller, *Complete Works of Andrew Fuller*, 4:472.

7

Fuller's influence on the life and ministry of Spurgeon

Spurgeon's admiration of Andrew Fuller

Spurgeon had a lifelong admiration of Andrew Fuller and considered Fuller "the greatest theologian"[1] of his century.

Fuller's influence on Spurgeon's theological understanding

As a young man, Spurgeon drew upon Fuller's writings to help shape his own spiritual understanding and theological thought. For example, Spurgeon carefully perused Fuller's writings for insight into the hidden dangers of Antinomianism. He declared in his diary on April 17, 1850, just before his sixteenth birthday, "Read some of 'Fuller upon Antinomianism.' My God, what a gulf is near me! I think I can say that I hate this religion…[i.e. Antinomianism]."[2]

In what were his formative years, Spurgeon also turned to Fuller's writings for encouragement while wrestling with those who derided

---

1 Cited in Gilbert Laws, *Andrew Fuller: Pastor, Theologian, Ropeholder* (London: Carey Press, 1942), 127.

2 *The Early Years*, 128. Antinomianism is the doctrine that it is not necessary for Christians to preach and/or obey the moral law of the Old Testament.

believer's baptism. Spurgeon drew great comfort from the example of Fuller's own life and testimony: "I was noting," he wrote, "when reading the life of good Andrew Fuller, that, after he had been baptized, some of the young men in the village were wont to mock him, asking him how he liked being dipped.... I could but notice that the scoff of a hundred years ago is just the scoff of today."[3]

This deep respect and admiration for Fuller never waned. Twenty-seven years later, in *Commenting and Commentaries*, Spurgeon cited two of Fuller's biblical commentaries and warmly recommended them to his readers. Regarding Fuller's commentary on the book of Revelation, a difficult apocalyptic book, Spurgeon's confidence in Fuller was clearly evident. He wrote: "Fuller is too judicious to run into speculations."[4] In commenting upon Fuller's treatment of Genesis, Spurgeon's admiration knew no bounds, as he asserted, "Weighty, judicious, and full of Gospel truth. One of the very best of discourses extant upon Genesis."[5]

A Calvinistic Baptist heritage

As a Calvinistic Baptist heritage helped to hone Spurgeon's own spirituality and theological thought, Andrew Fuller's devotion to God and Calvinistic theology also found its antecedent in John Bunyan and John Gill. In writing to a close friend, Fuller openly shared that he gained great help and insight from both Gill and Bunyan. He stated: "The principal writings with which I was first acquainted, were those of Bunyan, Gill and [John] Brine. I had read pretty much of Gill's *Body of Divinity*, and from many parts of it had received considerable instruction."[6]

Fuller, Spurgeon and the doctrines of grace

It is interesting to note that Fuller, because of his hyper-Calvinist upbringing, struggled with reconciling election with the free offer of the gospel. He initially questioned the theology of Bunyan, and others

---

3   *The Early Years*, 147.

4   *The Early Years*, 199.

5   *The Early Years*, 117.

6   Ryland, *The Work of Faith*, 58–59.

in the Puritan era of the seventeenth century, who held to the doctrines of grace and yet freely and passionately preached the gospel to all. He recorded his own personal struggles based upon his reading of Bunyan and other Puritan authors: "They all deal, as Bunyan did, in free invitations to sinners to come to Christ and be saved; the consistency of which with personal election I could not understand."[7] Fuller was also well acquainted with *Pilgrim's Progress* and other writings of Bunyan. As an example, he freely quoted Bunyan to rebut idle speculative theology.[8] He also addressed comments and theological issues that arose from Gill's writings.[9] It is clear, therefore, that Fuller was habitually and diligently perusing the writings of Bunyan and Gill.

In Fuller's *The Gospel Worthy of All Acceptation*, he definitively champions the biblical truth that there is no contradiction between election and human responsibility. One can tenaciously uphold Calvinism, yet boldly and unambiguously preach the gospel of Christ to all. This battle for upholding both God's sovereignty and man's responsibility would rage amongst the Baptists, not only in Fuller's day, but also in Spurgeon's day. Like Fuller, Spurgeon would continually be in the line of fire, with hyper-Calvinists (especially among the Strict and Particular Baptists) on one side and, on the other, supporters of Arminianism (that is the General Baptists), each in turn taking careful aim at Spurgeon. Spurgeon had much to learn by identifying with Fuller in the struggle to enunciate a balanced biblical theology.

Conclusion

If one were to ask Spurgeon who was the greatest Baptist influence on his life, ministry and writings, perhaps Spurgeon would turn around with a smile on his face, and say: "John Gill, the theologian, enlarged my mind; Andrew Fuller, the all-rounder, enhanced and enriched my ministry; but John Bunyan, that tinker of Bedford, encouraged my life, my very soul."

---

7 Ryland, *The Work of Faith*, 59.
8 Ryland, *The Work of Faith*, 55.
9 Ryland, *The Work of Faith*, 8, 42, 55.

8

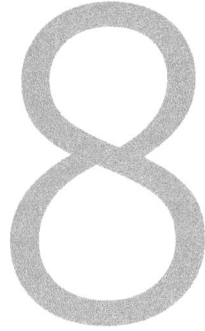

Spurgeon's advice to his students concerning personal spirituality

Introduction

C.H. Spurgeon considered personal spirituality a vital priority for ministers and ministerial students. Like Bunyan, Fuller and Gill before him, Spurgeon was convinced that ministerial success finds its genesis in personal spirituality.

To demonstrate the correlation between personal spirituality and ministerial success, this chapter concentrates on the presidential addresses and lectures Spurgeon delivered at the Pastors' College, which he founded in 1856, at the age of twenty-one. The chief resources for this section include: *An All-Round Ministry*, a collection of twelve annual addresses[1] out of a total of twenty-seven, *Lectures to My Students*, actual classroom lectures that Spurgeon delivered at the Pastors' College, and Spurgeon's final address—possibly his finest—delivered at the Pastors' College in April 1891, entitled *The Greatest Fight in the*

---

1 Delivered in 1872, 1874, 1875, 1877, 1880, 1881, 1882, 1886, 1887, 1888, 1889 and 1890.

World: C.H. Spurgeon's Final Manifesto. It was published separately after his death.

The Pastors' College

The Pastors' College commenced with one student, Thomas W. Medhurst (1834–1917), whom Spurgeon placed into the care of George Rogers (d.1891), a Congregational minister. Student numbers swiftly grew and Rogers was soon designated principal. In 1861, the classes moved into the newly-established Metropolitan Tabernacle located at the Elephant and Castle, South London. In 1874, premises to accommodate the growing student body were opened in Temple Street, behind the Metropolitan Tabernacle. Student residences were in private housing scattered around far and wide. The Pastors' College relocated in 1923 to Falkland Park, South Norwood, within half a mile of where Spurgeon had resided at "Westwood," now an all girls' school.[2]

The Pastors' College selected men who had already proved successful in a pulpit ministry over a minimum of two years. The college articulated the premise that it did not *make* preachers, but rather honed the students' existing skills and enriched their education. Spurgeon's purpose statement regarding the college would remain its focus throughout his life, to train preachers of the gospel of Christ. He emphatically declared, "If a student should learn a thousand things, and yet fail to preach the gospel acceptably, his College course will have missed its true design."[3] Spurgeon saw the training of gospel preachers as an absolute priority, as well as a great and glorious task. Spurgeon stated,

> No work can possibly confirm a greater benefit upon mankind than the training of ministers whom God has chosen, for around them spring up churches, schools, and all the agencies of religion and philanthropy. As we are commanded to pray for labourers in the Lord's harvest, so are we bound to prove the honesty of our prayers by our actions.[4]

---

2   Judy Powles, *Forward in Faith: Spurgeon's College in South Norwood* (Chelmsford, UK: Simmons Printers, n.d.), 1-9.

3   Spurgeon, *Lectures To My Students*, 1:iv.

4   Spurgeon, *Lectures To My Students*, 1:iv.

The Pastors' College

Contrary to perceived opinion that Spurgeon viewed the pulpit as the main priority in his ministry, his focus on the college was foremost in his thinking. Regarding the college he declared that it was his "life's labour and delight—a delight superior even to that afforded by my ministerial success."[5] Biographers such as Iain Murray who looked down through the corridors of time agreed with Spurgeon's insight that the Pastors' College proved to be his greatest contribution to Christendom.[6]

Emphasis on spirituality

Spurgeon was vigilant in the selection process for the Pastors' College. He stressed the need for personal spirituality as a prerequisite to admission. In the detailed description of the calibre of student, Spurgeon emphasized spirituality: "These are the men whom the Pastors' College welcomes. Men in whom spirituality, zeal, and the indwelling Spirit are to be found."[7] In addition to personal spirituality was the spiritual gift of proclamation: "[Students] need not fear refusal at our doors on account of poverty, if they possess those gifts of utterance which are essential to the preacher."[8] Spurgeon further affirmed that he had no intention of producing scholars, which was then as now in vogue, but rather preachers of the gospel. He avowed,

> The College aims at training preachers rather than scholars. To develop the faculty of ready speech, to help them to understand the word of God, and to foster the spirit of consecration, courage, and confidence in God, are objects so important that we put all other matters into a secondary position.[9]

Unlike many seminaries of Spurgeon's day that offered a multiplicity of theological systems, Spurgeon unashamedly affirmed that the Pastors' College was singular in theological focus. He acknowledged,

---

5   Cited by Iain H. Murray, "Introduction," in Spurgeon, *An All-Round Ministry*, i.
6   Iain H. Murray, "Introduction," in Spurgeon, *An All-Round Ministry*, i.
7   Spurgeon, *Lectures To My Students*, 1:iii–iv.
8   Spurgeon, *Lectures To My Students*, 1:iv.
9   Spurgeon, *Lectures To My Students*, 1:iv.

We hold by the doctrines of grace and the old orthodox faith, and have no sympathy with the countless theological novelties of the present day, which are novelties only in outward form: in substance they are repetitions of errors exploded long ago. Our standing in doctrinal matters is well known, and we make no profession of latitudinarian charity, yet we find no failure in the number of earnest spirits who rally to our standard, believing that in truth alone can true freedom be found.[10]

Exhortations to spirituality for ministerial success

The following extracts taken from *An All-Round Ministry* verify Spurgeon's conviction that spirituality is interrelated with ministerial success. In an address given to the Pastors' College in 1874 entitled "Forward," Spurgeon confirmed that ministerial success is directly linked to moral qualities. He tenaciously warned fellow ministers, like Bunyan, Gill and Fuller before him, that the converse also held true, namely, that moral failure leads to ministerial failure:

We desire to rise to the highest style of ministry; but even if we obtain the mental and oratorical qualifications I have mentioned, we shall fail, unless we also possess high moral qualities. There are evils which we must shake off, as Paul shook the viper from his hand, and there are virtues which we must gain at any cost.[11]

In this address, Spurgeon went on to cite a number of ministerial moral failures: self-indulgence, self-importance, self-adulation, poor control of one's temper and tendency to levity.[12] Spurgeon warned that without integrity a minister can accomplish very little: "He will never do much for God who has not integrity of spirit."[13] For Spurgeon, a deepened personal relationship with Christ is the only remedy for failure and the explanation of success:

---

10 Spurgeon, *Lectures To My Students*, 1:iv.
11 Spurgeon, *An All-Round Ministry*, 45–46.
12 Spurgeon, *An All-Round Ministry*, 46.
13 Spurgeon, *An All-Round Ministry*, 48.

Among spiritual acquirements, it is beyond all other things needful to know Him who is the sure remedy for all human diseases. Know Jesus. Sit at His feet. Consider His nature, His work, His sufferings, and His glory. Rejoice in His presence; commune with Him from day to day. To know Christ is to understand the most excellent of all sciences. You cannot fail to be wise if you commune with Incarnate Wisdom; you cannot lack strength if you have constant fellowship with God. Let this be your desire,

I would commune with Thee, my God;
  E'en to Thy seat I come;
I leave my joys, I leave my sins,
  And seek in Thee my home.

Dwell in God, brethren, not sometimes go to Him, but abide in Him.[14]

Spurgeon enthusiastically asserted that holiness is validated by ministerial success, not intellect or giftedness:

If we obtain conformity to Christ, we shall have a wondrous unction upon our ministry; and without that, what is a ministry worth? In a word, we must labour for holiness of character.... You must have holiness; and, dear brethren, if you should fail in mental qualifications (though I hope you will not), and if you should have a slender measure of the oratorical faculty (though I trust you will not), yet, depend upon it, a holy life is, in itself, a wonderful power, and will make up for many deficiencies; it is, in fact, the best sermon the best man can ever deliver. Let us resolve that all the purity which can be had we will have, that all the sanctity which can be reached we will obtain, and that all the likeness to Christ that is possible in this world of sin shall certainly be in us through the effectual working of the Spirit of God.

---

14 Spurgeon, *An All-Round Ministry*, 48.

The Lord lift us all, as a College, right up to a higher platform, and He shall have the glory![15]

In an address entitled "Individuality, and its Opposite," delivered in 1875 at the Pastors' College, Spurgeon once again emphasized the need for godliness in the life of a minister:

Personal godliness must never grow scanty with us. Our own personal justification in the righteousness of Christ, our personal sanctification by the indwelling power of the Holy Spirit, our vital union with Christ, and expectancy of glory in Him, yea, our own advancement in grace, or our own declension; all these we must well know and consider.[16]

Yet again, in an address entitled "A New Departure," which was delivered in 1880, the weapons of spirituality and the pursuit of holiness to combat the evils of the day are expounded by Spurgeon to the audience at the Pastors' College:

Surely our holy fellowship at this happy hour should help us all to rise to a higher level. The sight of many of our brethren is cheering and stimulating. When I remember concerning some their holiness, their depth of spirituality, their perseverance, I feel comforted in the belief that, if the Lord has strengthened others, He has yet a blessing in reserve for us also. Let this Feast of Tabernacles be the time for renewing our vows of consecration unto the Lord our God.[17]

Spurgeon relentlessly exhorted ministers and ministerial students to pursue truth, holiness and Christian grace. One sees this clearly in his address entitled "Stewards," delivered in 1887, where he expounds on the danger of conniving evil:

---

15 Spurgeon, *An All-Round Ministry*, 53.
16 Spurgeon, *An All-Round Ministry*, 64.
17 Spurgeon, *An All-Round Ministry*, 154.

Yield in all things personal, but be firm where truth and holiness are concerned. We must be faithful, lest we incur the sin and penalty of Eli. Be honest to the rich and influential; be firm with the wavering and unsteady; for the blood of these will be required at our hand. Brothers, you will need all the wisdom and grace you can get in order to fulfill your duties as pastors.[18]

In 1888, the Down-Grade Controversy was in full swing. Here Spurgeon urges those before him to stand firm and resist a spirit to compromise not only in truth but in personal integrity:

Are not important persons too much consulted? Is not position more valued than spirituality? Is there enough of downright faithfulness to truth and to Christ at all hazards? Brethren, we want grace to say, "I can be poor; I can be ridiculed; I can be abused; but I cannot be false to my Lord." I make no personal reference, but I see the spirit of compromise concerning holiness and sin, truth and error, far too prevalent. The spirit of compromise comes not of the Spirit of God, but of the spirit of the world.[19]

In Spurgeon's 1889 address "The Preacher's Power and the Conditions of Obtaining It," we can see his conviction that blessing and power associated with ministerial success flow not from gifts or talents but from an intimate walk with God. He declared:

Above all, dear friends, if you want the blessing of God, keep up constant communion with God.... If we always walk with God, and act towards Him as children towards a loving father, so that the spirit of adoption is always in us, and the spirit of love always flows forth from us, we shall preach with power, and God will bless our ministry: for then we shall know and utter the mind of God. I must add here that, if we are to enjoy the power of God, we must manifest great holiness of life.... But we must have

---

18 Spurgeon, *An All-Round Ministry*, 277.
19 Spurgeon, *An All-Round Ministry*, 291.

holiness to a high degree. Unholy living! How can God bless it?[20]

There is no doubt in Spurgeon's mind and heart that ministerial spirituality is essential for power and blessing in ministry. Understandably this was an ongoing plea to fellow ministers.

Lectures to My Students
The following extracts are taken from Spurgeon's *Lectures to My Students*, delivered to students at the Pastors' College.

In his first lecture, "The Minister's Self Watch," based on "Take heed unto thyself, and unto the doctrine" (1 Timothy 4:16), Spurgeon impressed upon his students that agencies and ministries are useless if the cultivation of personal spirituality is ignored. He solemnly declared,

> It will be in vain for me to stock my library, or organize societies, or project schemes, if I neglect the culture of myself; for books, and agencies, and systems, are only remotely the instruments of my holy calling; my own spirit, soul, and body, are my nearest machinery for sacred service; my spiritual faculties, and my inner life, are my battle ax and weapons of war.[21]

Spurgeon goes on to stress the necessity of a minister's spirituality by quoting from the well-known Scottish preacher Robert Murray McCheyne (1813–1843):

> M'Cheyne, writing to a ministerial friend, who was travelling with a view to perfecting himself in the German tongue, used language identical with our own:—"I know you will apply hard to German, but do not forget the culture of the inner man—I mean of the heart. How diligently the cavalry officer keeps his saber clean and sharp; every stain he rubs off with the greatest care. Remember you are God's sword, his instrument—I trust, a chosen vessel unto him to bear his name. In great measure,

---

20 Spurgeon, *An All-Round Ministry*, 350.

21 Spurgeon, *Lectures To My Students*, 1:2.

according to the purity and perfection of the instrument, will be the success. It is not great talents God blesses so much as likeness to Jesus. A holy minister is an awful weapon in the hand of God."[22]

Spurgeon insisted that a holy life is an attractive life and draws men to Christ like a magnet. All ministers, according to Spurgeon, who yearn for souls, must excel in the pursuit of spirituality. They are to be men of God, men after God's own heart, men that seek God's glory alone.

In another lecture, Spurgeon focuses on spirituality in prayer. Here, in the lecture entitled "The Preacher's Private Prayer," Spurgeon emphasizes the necessity of a life devoted to prayer. Prayer, according to Spurgeon, is essential for powerful and successful preaching. He declared, "Prayer will singularly assist you in the delivery of your sermon; in fact, nothing can so gloriously fit you to preach as descending fresh from the mount of communion with God to speak with men."[23] The converse is also true. A minister that neglects the spirituality of prayer is sure to fail. Spurgeon warned his students,

If you as ministers are not very prayerful, you are much to be pitied. If, in the future, you shall be called to sustain pastorates, large or small, if you become lax in secret devotion, not only will you need to be pitied, but your people also; and, in addition to that, you shall be blamed, and the day cometh in which you shall be ashamed and confounded.[24]

Spurgeon cites David Brainerd (1718–1747) as an example of spirituality in prayer and ministerial success. Spurgeon affirmed, "Could any one wonder at Brainerd's success, when his diary contains such notes as this: "Lord's Day, April 25th—This morning spent about two hours in sacred duties, and was enabled, more than ordinarily, to agonize for immortal souls; though it was early in the morning, and the sun scarcely shone at all, yet my body was quite wet with sweat."[25]

---

22 Spurgeon, *Lectures To My Students*, 1:2.
23 Spurgeon, *Lectures To My Students*, 1:43.
24 Spurgeon, *Lectures To My Students*, 1:41.
25 Spurgeon, *Lectures To My Students*, 1:45.

Again, Spurgeon cites Martin Luther (1483–1546) as a man whose prayer life was the key reason for his ministerial success. Spurgeon impressed upon his students, "The secret of Luther's power lay in the same direction." Spurgeon points out that someone overheard the intimate communion of Luther with God and stated, "I overheard him in prayer, but, good God, with what life and spirit did he pray! It was with so much reverence, as if he were speaking to God, yet with so much confidence as if he were speaking to his friend." Spurgeon concluded, "My brethren, let me beseech you to be men of prayer. Great talents you may never have, but you will do well enough without them if you abound in intercession."[26]

In another lecture entitled "The Holy Spirit in Connection With Our Ministry," Spurgeon points out that sin grieves the Holy Spirit and therefore hinders the success of ministry: "We cannot expect the Spirit of God to bless a ministry which never ought to have been exercised, and certainly a graceless ministry is of that character."[27]

The Greatest Fight in the World

The Greatest Fight in the World: C.H. Spurgeon's Final Manifesto was the last inaugural address delivered by Spurgeon at the Pastors' College Conference in April 1891. His theme was "the good fight of faith" taken from 1 Timothy 6:12. He exhorted fellow ministers and students to do their best in the service of their King. Published after Spurgeon's death, without doubt, it is recognized as one of the most forceful addresses ever delivered by Spurgeon. Here, we unmistakably see Spurgeon's unwavering conviction that holiness lies at the root of the gospel, its proclamation and its ultimate success. Spurgeon boldly asserts, "The very root of holiness lies in the gospel of our Lord Jesus Christ."[28] He affirms that the doctrines of grace produce spirituality: "We have seen a fine morality, a stern integrity, a delicate purity, and, what is more, a devout holiness, produced by the doctrines of grace."[29]

---

26 Spurgeon, *Lectures To My Students*, 1:45.

27 Spurgeon, *Lectures To My Students*, 2:19.

28 C.H. Spurgeon, *The Greatest Fight in the World: C.H. Spurgeon's Final Manifesto* (1891; reprint, Albany: Ages Software, 1998), 9.

29 Spurgeon, *The Greatest Fight in the World*, 9.

Like Bunyan, Spurgeon was convicted that ministers must cultivate inner spirituality through the prayerful study of God's Word. He believed this was not only an act of devotion but an act of transforming grace. "The prayerful study of the Word is not only a means of instruction, but an act of devotion wherein the transforming power of grace is often exercised, changing us into the image of him of whom the Word is a mirror."[30] Spurgeon insisted that the study of God's Word must be with an open heart. He cites as examples the evangelical giants of old. He declared,

> Is there anything, after all, like the Word of God when the open books find open hearts? When I read the lives of such men as Baxter, Brainerd, McCheyne, and many others, why, I feel like one who has bathed himself in some cool brook after having gone a journey through a black country, which left him dusty and depressed.[31]

A life bathed in Scripture becomes a living testimony. Again, Spurgeon emphasized the Word to cultivate spirituality, and he impressed upon his students and ministers, "…such men embodied Scripture in their lives and illustrated it in their experience. The washing of water by the Word is what they had, and what we need."[32]

Spurgeon not only saw the Word of God shaping the minister's spirituality but also the important role of the church in prayer. Spurgeon stated, "If a church is to be what it ought to be for the purposes of God, we must train it in the holy art of prayer."[33] Indeed, Spurgeon attributed gospel success directly to the prayer meeting. The converse was also true; lack of power in the ministry often finds its antecedent in lack of prayer in the church. Spurgeon sounded the alarm when he declared, "Churches without prayer-meetings are grievously common…. In many churches the prayer-meeting is only the skeleton of

30 Spurgeon, *The Greatest Fight in the World*, 12.
31 Spurgeon, *The Greatest Fight in the World*, 12.
32 Spurgeon, *The Greatest Fight in the World*, 12.
33 Spurgeon, *The Greatest Fight in the World*, 28.

a gathering: the form is kept up, but the people do not come."[34] He urged fellow ministers and students to train their people to pray earnestly: "Oh, my brothers, let it not be so with you! Do train the people to continually meet together for prayer. Rouse them to incessant supplication." Spurgeon unequivocally declared, "Believe me, if a church does not pray, it is dead. Instead of putting united prayer last, put it first. Everything will hinge upon the power of prayer in the church."[35]

Spurgeon saw the essential need of the church to reproduce. In so doing he lists the characteristics of a healthy vibrant church not by size but by spirituality. Again he emphasized personal spirituality: "Brethren, we want churches also that produce saints; men of mighty faith and prevalent prayer; men of holy living, and of consecrated giving; men filled with the Holy Spirit."[36]

In Spurgeon's thinking, true spirituality must be the foundation of all churches. Spurgeon affirmed, "I would desire to see in every church a Mary sitting at Jesus' feet, a Martha serving Jesus, a Peter and a John; but the best name for a church is 'All Saints.' All believers should be saints, and all may be saints. Oh, for more of them!"[37]

Once more Spurgeon reaffirms to his audience that the key to ministerial success is spirituality, "If God shall so help us that the whole company of the faithful shall, each one of them individually, come to the fulness of the stature of a man in Christ Jesus, then we shall see greater things than these. Glorious times will come when believers have glorious characters."[38]

If holiness lies at the root of a successful ministry, then the opposite is also true: that sin may lie at the root of a failed ministry. Spurgeon directly links unsanctified ministers with ministerial failure.

We are to be examples to our flock in all things. In all diligence, in all gentleness, in all humility, and in all holiness we are to excel....We cannot expect to see holy churches if we who are

34 Spurgeon, *The Greatest Fight in the World*, 28.
35 Spurgeon, *The Greatest Fight in the World*, 29.
36 Spurgeon, *The Greatest Fight in the World*, 29.
37 Spurgeon, *The Greatest Fight in the World*, 29.
38 Spurgeon, *The Greatest Fight in the World*, 29.

bound to be their examples are unsanctified. If there be, in any of our brethren, consecration and sanctification, evident to all men, God has blessed them, and God will bless them more and more. If these be lacking in us, we need not search far to find the cause of our non-success.[39]

Spurgeon again underscores the necessity of holiness in the life of the minister:

Next, remember that the Holy Ghost will never sanction sin; and to bless the ministry of some men would be to sanction their evil ways. "Be ye clean, that bear the vessels of the Lord." Let your character correspond with your teaching, and let your churches be purged from open transgressors, lest the Holy Ghost disown your teaching, not for its own sake, but because of the ill savour of unholy living which dishonours it.[40]

Spurgeon concluded this potent address as he encouraged ministers to lead their godly flock in the power of the Holy Spirit:

Go forth with the companies of the godly whom you lead, and let every man be strong in the Lord, and in the power of his might. As men alive from the dead, go forth in the quickening power of the Holy Ghost: you have no other strength. May the blessing of the Triune God rest upon you, one and all, for the Lord Jesus Christ's sake! Amen.[41]

We will close this section with a poem written by Spurgeon to young ministers:

---

39 Spurgeon, *The Greatest Fight in the World*, 32.
40 Spurgeon, *The Greatest Fight in the World*, 41.
41 Spurgeon, *The Greatest Fight in the World*, 43.

TO A YOUNG MINISTER,
"*A good minister of Jesus Christ*"—1 Timothy 4:6

The Lord Jesus Christ with thy spirit be:
Thee may his presence gladden, help, defend:
Him serve with all thy powers continually:
His glory seek, and on his love depend.

The work is thine, to lead mankind to God;
On Christ's behalf, with sinful men to plead;
To point them to the sin-atoning blood;
With quickening, saving truth their souls to feed.

"Watch thou in all things;" "to thyself take heed;"
Claim all the blessings through the Saviour given;
A Christian be in heart, in word, in deed;
Live as becomes "an heir of God" and heaven.

Be it thy care as much of Christ to know
As heart can feel, as spirit can conceive;
And strive his love and preciousness to show,
That men in him may savingly believe.

And by thy means, through his abundant grace,
May many souls from sin and death be won;
And mayest thou stand with joy before his face,
And see him smile, and hear him say, "WELL DONE."[42]

---

42 C.H. Spurgeon, "To a young minister," *The Sword and the Trowel*, 1879 [Ed. note: this reference is unverified].

9

C.H. Spurgeon's personal spirituality

Introduction

This chapter focuses on Spurgeon's personal spirituality. His inner life is examined through a number of windows. For example, his spirituality in devotion to God is examined through his rendering of psalms and hymns in his hymnal, *Our Own Hymn-Book*. We also glean insight regarding Spurgeon's "inner-life" from his pulpit prayers, which are set forth in *C.H. Spurgeon's Prayers*, which further reveal his love and devotion to God. An examination of *The Metropolitan Tabernacle Pulpit* reveals that Spurgeon's preaching is saturated with expressions of uninhibited love and intense devotion to Christ, expressed in the pursuit of spirituality. Spurgeon's virtuous relationship with his wife and immediate family is also examined. This aspect of his life is gleaned from *The Letters of C.H. Spurgeon* as well as in his *Autobiography*. Finally, Spurgeon's works of mercy spanning his lifetime are evaluated.

Spirituality in hymnology

Spurgeon's hymnal grants valuable insight into his personal spirituality, unbridled worship, passionate devotion and humble adoration of God. Spurgeon earnestly yearned to promote and uphold biblical worship among his people at the Metropolitan Tabernacle. With this in mind, he published a new hymnal entitled *Our Own Hymn-Book* in 1866. The hymnal, compiled by Spurgeon himself, constituted a body of psalms and hymns in excess of 1,060, and was reflective of a Puritan Calvinistic heritage. Spurgeon contributed a rendering of fifteen Psalms, as well as writing fourteen hymns.[1]

An analysis of Spurgeon's rendering of the psalms revealed his deep theological devotion and profound reverence to his great and glorious Lord. As an example, in Psalm 15, the character of those who may dwell with the Lord is developed. Spurgeon in his rendering of the psalm revealed his yearning to be conformed to the will of his great, holy God. First, utilizing eleven pronouns over six stanzas, Spurgeon personalized the psalm to ensure full impact and import to his own life and the lives of others. Second, he pleads with God that he be conformed more to his will:

Lord, I would dwell with Thee
　On Thy most holy hill;
Oh, shed Thy grace abroad in me,
　To mould me to Thy will.

The pursuit of spirituality is clearly expressed:

Oh, tame my tongue to peace,
　And tune my heart to love;
From all reproaches may I cease,
　Made harmless as a dove.

The vile, though proudly great,
　No flatterer find in me;
I count Thy saints of poor estate
　Far nobler company.

---

1   See C.H. Spurgeon, comp., *Our Own Hymn-Book: A Collection of Psalms and Hymns for Public, Social, and Private Worship* (1866; reprint, Pasadena: Pilgrim Publications, 2002): Psalms 15, 21, 30, 39, 41, 44, 53, 58, 60, 70, 82, 83, 111, 112 and 120; hymns 451, 632, 897, 904, 923, 934, 939, 974, 1020, 1022, 1055, 1056, 1058 and 1059.

Again he pleads for spirituality:

> Faithful, but meekly kind,
>   Gentle, yet boldly true,
> I would possess the perfect mind
>   Which in my Lord I view.

In concluding the rendering of this psalm, Spurgeon clearly yearned for Christlikeness:

> But, Lord, these graces all
>   Thy Spirit's work must be:
> To Thee, through Jesus' blood I call—
>   Create them all in me.[2]

In Psalm 21 Spurgeon rejoiced as he expounded the theme of the kingship of Christ. In so doing he presented the glory of Christ before his congregation as one who is triumphant and therefore worthy of all praise and adoration. He wrote:

> Thy strength, O Lord, makes glad our King…
> His royal pomp all heaven admires;
>   Thou on His head has set the crown.[3]

Spurgeon concludes with joy, wonder and awe, as he sees his Lord high and lifted up:

> Be Thou exalted, King of kings
>   In Thine own strength sit Thou on high,
> Thy church Thy triumph loudly sings,
>   And lauds Thy glorious majesty.[4]

---

2 Spurgeon, *Our Own Hymn-Book*, 3.
3 Spurgeon, *Our Own Hymn-Book*, 5.
4 Spurgeon, *Our Own Hymn-Book*, 5.

Again, as he rendered Psalm 82, Spurgeon exalted the sovereign King. He declared,

> The kings of the earth are in the hands
>   Of God who reigns on high;
> He in their council-chamber stands,
>   And sees with watchful eye.[5]

Spurgeon readily proclaimed the wonder of Christ's glorious salvation to sinners such as himself. He wrote in his rendering of Psalm 30:

> My sins have brought me near the grave,
>   The grave of black despair;
> I look'd but there was none to save
>   Till I looked up in prayer.

He gratefully acknowledged in the psalm that Christ alone saved him from the terrors of hell:

> In answer to my piteous cries,
>   From hell's dark brink I'm brought:
> My Jesus saw me from the skies,
>   And swift salvation wrought.[6]

Spurgeon fully realized that it was all of grace. That grace alone saved and preserved. His pursuit of spirituality caused a hate towards sin and a plea for God's restraining hand. This is clear as he penned in his rendering of Psalm 58:

> O God, Thou judgest all the earth,
>   Thy justice cheers my cleansed heart;
> Restrain my soul from sinner's mirth,
>   Lest in their doom I bear a part.[7]

---

5   Spurgeon, *Our Own Hymn-Book*, 22.

6   Spurgeon, *Our Own Hymn-Book*, 7.

7   Spurgeon, *Our Own Hymn-Book*, 16.

Despite numerous trials, Spurgeon was ever conscious and confident that God was at hand. Based on Psalm 39, Spurgeon joyfully asserts:

> Though I'm exiled from glory's land,
> Yet not from glory's King;
> My God is ever near at hand,
> And therefore I will sing.[8]

Again in Psalm 44 we hear Spurgeon's battle cry as he proclaimed that the church's strength and confidence was in God alone:

> From grace alone their strength shall spring,
> Nor bow, nor sword can save;
> To God alone, their Lord and King
> Shall all their banners wave.[9]

Again, in Psalm 60, we sense Spurgeon's passion as he triumphantly writes:

> Through Thee we shall most valiant prove,
> And tread the foes beneath our feet;
> Through Thee our faith shall hills remove,
> And small as chaff the mountains beat.[10]

We conclude this brief overview of Spurgeon's rendition of the psalms with his rendering of Psalm 11. Again we observe and confirm his genuine spirituality expressed in heartfelt adoration of his Lord:

> Praise the Lord with exaltation
> My whole heart my Lord shall praise
> 'Midst the upright congregation,
> Loftiest Hallelujahs raise.

---

8 Spurgeon, *Our Own Hymn-Book*, 10.

9 Spurgeon, *Our Own Hymn-Book*, 11.

10 Spurgeon, *Our Own Hymn-Book*, 16.

Therefore be His praise unceasing,
    Be His name for ever blessed;
And with confidence increasing,
    Let us on His promise rest.[11]

Spirituality in all spheres of pastoral ministry

Spurgeon tenaciously believed that every sphere of pastoral ministry must be seen as an act of spirituality. It is therefore noteworthy that a number of hymns penned by Spurgeon centre around pastoral duties; namely, hymns that guided and enriched the congregation in the prayer meeting, choice of office bearers, ministry at the ordinances of baptism and the Lord's table.

Spurgeon was no armchair theologian. He remained on the front-line, battling in various areas throughout his life. Without question he leaned heavily and hard upon the Holy Spirit to draw strength and power to preach, teach, pray and pursue a sanctified life. It is thus not by accident that his first hymn is dedicated to the person and ministry of the Holy Spirit. In his hymn of thanks and adoration, Spurgeon ascribes glory and honour to him. The terms he chose express this adoration: majesty, reigns, indwells, comforts, adored, obeyed, power, life, hope and blessed.

This hymn appears to be written for the prayer meeting. Its theme is the presence of the Spirit of God:

The Holy Ghost is here,
    Where saints in prayer agree…

Not far away is He,
    To be by prayer brought nigh,
But here in present majesty…

He dwells within our soul,
    An ever welcome Guest;
He reigns with absolute control,
    As Monarch in the breast.

---

11 Spurgeon, *Our Own Hymn-Book*, 31–32.

Our bodies are His shrine,
  And He th' indwelling Lord.
All hail, Thou Comforter divine,
  Be evermore Adored!

Obedient to thy will,
  We wait to feel Thy power,
O Lord of life, our hope fulfil,
  And bless this hallowed hour.[12]

A further example comes from the appointing of office bearers. Spurgeon wrote two hymns to guide the congregation as they drew near to God for wisdom and guidance.[13] The first hymn petitioned God as it pled for a minister. The second hymn petitioned God for guidance as office bearers are selected from among the congregation. Spurgeon's pious zeal wanted God's man; not a man of mere eloquence or affluence, but a man after God's own heart. He wrote:

Risen Lord, Thou hast received
  Gifts to bless the sons of men....

Now these gifts be pleased to bless us,
  Elders, Deacons, still supply,
Men whom Thou art pleased to lend us,
  All the saints to edify.

Guide us when we select them
  Let the Holy Ghost be nigh,
Do Thou, Lord, Thyself elect them,
  And ordain them from on high.

[Pause while the election is made]

---

12 Spurgeon, *Our Own Hymn-Book*, 106.
13 Hymns 897, 904.

Pour on them Thy rich anointing,
Fill Thy servants with Thy power,
Prove them of Thy own appointing,
Bless them from this very hour.[14]

Spurgeon's spirituality in baptism is also evident.[15] Note how he weaves the identification of the believer with his Saviour:

Here we behold the grave
Which held our buried Head;
We claim a burial in the wave
Because with Jesus dead.

Here too we see Him rise,
And live no more to die;
And one with Him by sacred ties
We rise to live on high.[16]

Spurgeon's devotion in ministerial practice is further evident at the Lord's table. For this ordinance, Spurgeon wrote five hymns; three for before the meal,[17] and two for after the meal.[18] The first call upon the presence and blessing of God, while the latter offer thanksgiving.

We close this section with a quote from one of these communion hymns. It illustrates Spurgeon's abounding love and devotion to a felt Christ, the crucified one:

Amidst us our Beloved stands,
And bids us view His pierced hands;
Points to His wounded feet and side,
Blessed emblems of the crucified.

---

14 Spurgeon, *Our Own Hymn-Book*, 197.
15 See hymns 923 and 934.
16 Spurgeon, *Our Own Hymn-Book*, 208.
17 See hymns 939, 1055 and 1056.
18 See hymns 1058, 1059.

Thou glorious Bridegroom of our hearts,
  Thy present smile a heaven imparts:
O lift the veil, if veil there be,
  Let every saint Thy beauties see.[19]

Spirituality in prayer

As we examine Spurgeon's pulpit prayers, we are conscious that we tread on holy ground. The Lord Jesus said, "For out of the abundance of the heart the mouth speaks" (Matthew 12:34, NKJV). In evaluating these expressions of the soul, we gain insight into the innermost being of Spurgeon: his holy devotion, his healthy character, his hatred towards sin, his humility, his passion for souls, his hope of glory and his fear of hell. Nothing reaches more into the depths of our being and reveals more of our soul's deepest yearnings and passions than our prayers, both public and private. *C.H. Spurgeon's Prayers* reveals not only Spurgeon's own great devotion and pursuit of holiness but also his burden for his people who had been entrusted to his pastoral care by God's sovereign grace.

John Cairns (1818–1892), who is cited in the introduction of *C.H. Spurgeon's Prayers*, stated:

Prayer was the instinct of his soul, and the atmosphere of his life. It was his "vital breath" and "native air." How naturally he inhaled and exhaled it! The greatness of his prayers more and more impresses and delights me. He touched every note. He sped as on eagle's wings, into the Heaven of God.[20]

Dinsdale T. Young (1861–1938), a Methodist minister and eyewitness to Spurgeon's spirituality, points out:

Precious to him beyond compare was the Divine Redeemer. The blood of our redemption was his glory. The atoning cross was all in all to him.[21]

---

19 Spurgeon, *Our Own Hymn-Book*, 204–205.

20 John Cairns, cited in "Introduction," in *C.H. Spurgeon's Prayers* (1905; reprint, Grand Rapids: Baker Book House, 1981), i.

21 Dinsdale T. Young, "Introduction," in *C.H. Spurgeon's Prayers*, iii.

Spurgeon's prayers unequivocally demonstrate his own personal spirituality and his yearning for the flame of sacred devotion to God among his people. There is, in the prayers, a holy expectation that God would promote personal spirituality within the hearts of those in the congregation as an answer to numerous passionate petitions that Spurgeon would earnestly address to God.

In general, Spurgeon's prayers are triune in nature, theologically astute in character and passionate in fervour. Public and private prayers are inevitably yoked together, as Dinsdale T. Young observes: "How naturally prayer fell from the lips of that great Apostle! We felt that he was only doing before the multitude what he was habituated to do in private."[22] Young further points out Spurgeon's evident passion, pursuit and pleasure of God:

> These noble prayers will be seen to be full of theology. They were the utterances of one who studied God, delighted in God, and walked with God, especially with the God-man.[23]

Pursuit of worship

Spurgeon's prayers overflowed with worship to the triune God. In the prayer "Thanks Be unto God," we see that Spurgeon was very conscious of the triune nature of God:

> We worship the Father, we worship the Son, we worship the Holy Ghost with all the powers of our being. We fall prostrate before the awful yet glorious throne of the Infinite Majesty of heaven. The Lord accept us since we offer these praises in the name of Jesus.[24]

Worship permeated all of Spurgeon's prayers. To Spurgeon, prayer was an act of worship. In "To the King Eternal," he commences his prayer with unbridled love and devotion to God:

---

22 *C.H. Spurgeon's Prayers*, vi.

23 *C.H. Spurgeon's Prayers*, viii.

24 *C.H. Spurgeon's Prayers*, 9.

We would begin with adoration. We worship from our hearts the Three in One, the infinite glorious Jehovah, the only living and true God. We adore the Father, the Son, and the Holy Ghost, the God of Abraham, of Isaac, and of Jacob. We are not yet ascended to the place where pure spirits behold the face of God, but we shall soon be there, perhaps much sooner than we think, and we would be there in spirit right now, casting our crowns upon the glassy sea before the throne of the Infinite Majesty and ascribing glory and honour, and power and praise, and dominion and might to Him that sitteth upon the throne, and unto the Lamb forever and ever. All the Church doth worship Thee, O God, every heart renewed by grace takes a delight in adoring Thee, and we, among the rest, though least and meanest of them all, yet would bow as heartily as any, worshipping, loving, praising, in our soul, being silent unto God because our joy in Him is altogether inexpressible.[25]

He often concluded his prayers with explicit acts of worship as in "Thanks be unto God":

Reign, Immanuel, reign; sit on the high throne; ride on Thy White Horse; and let the armies of heaven follow thee, conquering and to conquer. Come, Lord Jesus; even so, come quickly. Amen and amen.[26]

Pursuit of holiness
Spurgeon longed to be conformed to God's will in perfect obedience. This is clearly apparent in his prayer entitled "Help from on High":

Lord sanctify us. Oh! that Thy Spirit would come and saturate every faculty, subdue every passion, and use every power of our nature for obedience to God. Come, Holy Spirit, we do know Thee; Thou hast often overshadowed us. Come, more fully take possession of us.[27]

---

25 *C.H. Spurgeon's Prayers*, 25–26.
26 *C.H. Spurgeon's Prayers*, 11.
27 *C.H. Spurgeon's Prayers*, 3.

We can hear the cry from Spurgeon's heart as he earnestly pleads with God for consecration:

> Come, more fully take possession of us. Standing now as we do before the mercy seat our very highest prayer is for perfect holiness, complete consecration, entire cleansing from every evil. Take our heart, our head, our hands, our feet and use us all for thee.[28]

> Lord, keep us all from sin; teach us how to walk circumspectly; enable us to guard our minds against error of doctrine, our hearts against wrong feelings, and our lives against evil actions. Oh, may we never speak unadvisedly with our lips, nor give way to anger. Above all, keep us from covetousness which is idolatry, and from malice which is of the devil.[29]

Pursuit of a consecrated lifestyle

Spurgeon was not one who sought pleasure apart from God. His life was dedicated and consecrated in service to God. All that he did revolved around his passion for God and the gospel of Christ. This included providential blessings such as economic wealth and talent. Everything, in Spurgeon's mind, must be fully consecrated to God. Thus we hear him asking God:

> Lord, take our substance, let us not hoard it for ourselves, nor spend it for ourselves. Take our talent, let us not try to educate ourselves that we may have the repute of being wise, but let every gain of mental attainment be still that we may serve Thee better.... May we sanctify the world for your service. May we be lumps of salt in the midst of society.[30]

Pursuit of the lost

Spurgeon passionately prayed for those outside of Christ. Listen to him as he pleads at length for the non-Christian:

---

28 "Help from on high" in *C.H. Spurgeon's Prayers*, 3–4.
29 "Thanks be unto God" in *C.H. Spurgeon's Prayers*, 10–11.
30 *C.H. Spurgeon's Prayers*, 4.

And now most blessed Lord, look down upon those who do not love Thee. O Redeemer, look upon them with those eyes of Thine, which are as flames of fire. Let them see how ill they treat Thee. May they consider within themselves how dire is the ingratitude which can be negligent of a Saviour's blood, indifferent from a Saviour's heart. Oh, bring the careless and the godless to seek for mercy. Let those that are postponing serious things begin to see that the very thought of postponement of the claims of Christ is treason against His Majesty. O Saviour, dart Thine arrows abroad and let them wound many that they may fall down before Thee and cry out for mercy.[31]

In the "All-Prevailing Plea," Spurgeon again cries out to God for the lost. He declares:

Oh! that we could pour out our soul in prayer for the unconverted! Thou knowest where they will all be in a few years! Oh! by Thy wrath, we pray Thee, Let them not endure it! By the flames of hell, be pleased to ransom them from going down into the pit! By everything that is dreadful in the wrath to come we do argue with Thee to have mercy upon these sons of men, even upon those who have no mercy upon themselves.[32]

Spirituality in preaching

Spurgeon's preaching is characterized by a call to holiness. According to Spurgeon, a life lived in the presence of the holy God must be characterized by a life of spirituality. In fact, without the earnest ongoing pursuit of spirituality, Spurgeon would question the validity of one's profession of faith.

In Spurgeon's mind, spirituality involved a dread of sin before a holy God. In a sermon delivered by the young Spurgeon on April 8, 1855, before a packed audience at Exeter Hall, Spurgeon expounded on the text, "Come, see the place where the Lord lay" (Matthew 28:6). In the sermon Spurgeon takes great pains to drive home the heinous nature

---

31 *C.H. Spurgeon's Prayers,* 9–10.
32 *C.H. Spurgeon's Prayers,* 23.

of personal sin. He left those who heard him in no doubt that it was their sin that crucified Christ. Consequently, emotions of deep sorrow for sin are appropriate. He boldly declared:

> First, I would bid you stand and see the place where the Lord lay with emotions of deep sorrow. O come, my beloved brother, thy Jesus once lay there. He was a murdered man, my soul, and thou the murderer.

> Ah, you, my sins, my cruel sins,
>   His chief tormentors were,
> Each of my crimes became a nail,
>   And unbelief the spear.

> Alas! and did my Saviour bleed?
>   And did my Sovereign die?

> I slew him—this right hand struck the dagger to his heart. My deeds slew Christ. Alas! I slew my best beloved; I killed him who loved me with an everlasting love. Ye eyes, why do ye refuse to weep when ye see Jesus' body mangled and torn?[33]

Some years later, in 1862, at the Metropolitan Tabernacle, Spurgeon laid hold of his congregation as he expounded from Hebrews 12:14: "Holiness, without which no man shall see the Lord." Here Spurgeon calls the whole congregation to holiness and spares no one who secretly delighted in sin. In fact, Spurgeon solemnly warned that where there is no genuine pursuit of spirituality there is no authentic salvation. The pursuit of spirituality is not optional for the believer. He gravely said:

> And I am quite sure that you know nothing of true holiness if you can look forward to any future indulgence of sensual appetites with a certain degree of delightful anticipation. Have I a man here, a professed Christian, who has formed some design in his

---

33 "The Tomb of Jesus" in *The New Park Street Pulpit*, 1:133.

Metropolitan Tabernacle

mind to indulge the flesh, and to enjoy forbidden dainties when an opportunity occurs? Ah, sir! if thou canst think of those things that may come in thy way without tremor, I suspect thee: I would thou wouldst suspect thyself.[34]

In the same sermon, Spurgeon argues for uniformity of holiness both public and private. In his mind, a person's actions and demeanour in public should correspond to their actions in private. He sees home life as a truer yardstick in the pursuit of spirituality than that of public life. In this regard, according to his sons' testimony, which we will see later, Spurgeon lived out what he preached. Leaving no stone unturned, he drives home the pursuit of genuine spirituality to each member of his congregation:

> Again, methinks you have great cause for questioning, unless your holiness is uniform; I mean, if your life is angelic abroad and devilish at home. You must suspect that it is at home that you are what you really are. I question whether any man is much better than he is thought to be by his wife and family, for they, after all, see the most of us, and know the truth about us; and if, sir, though you seem in the pulpit, or on the platform, or in the shop, to be amiable, Christian, and God-like to the passer-by, your children should have to mark your unkindness, your want of fatherly affection for their souls, and your wife has to complain of your domineering, of the absence of everything that is Christ-like, you may shrewdly suspect that there is something wrong in the state of your heart. O sirs, true holiness is a thing that will keep by night and by day, at home and abroad, on the land and on the sea![35]

Spurgeon saw an entire congregation pursuing spirituality as a glorious testimony of the gospel to a fallen humanity. In a sermon preached on April 28, 1872, to his congregation at the Metropolitan Tabernacle from the text of 1 Thessalonians 1:5–10, Spurgeon urged:

---

34 "Holiness Demanded" in *The Metropolitan Tabernacle Pulpit*, 50:462.
35 "Holiness Demanded" in *The Metropolitan Tabernacle Pulpit*, 50:463.

The Church at Thessalonica sounded forth the gospel involuntarily, and also voluntarily. They did it involuntarily, for their very lives spake. If they did not preach, they were so full of faith, and good works, and holiness, that other people talked about it, and the matter was known, and the work of God in the hearts of the Church could be perceived in the lives of the members, and so it went out. Oh! how happy should any pastor be whose people should be so godly, so united, so generous, so persevering, so prayerful, so full of faith and of the Holy Ghost, that everywhere they should be spoken of, and through them, through their conduct, the Word of God should be sounded abroad. See to that, my brethren—see to it. God has placed us where we are observed of many. Give them something to observe worth seeing. With the eyes of a multitude of witnesses upon us, let us run with patience—the race that is set before us.[36]

Spirituality in relationships

What was Spurgeon really like? An analysis of his personal correspondence grants us further insight into his spirituality. This section examines Spurgeon's letters and relationship with his family and friends.

1. Spirituality in relations with parents

As a young man, Spurgeon freely shared his intimate love and devotion to Christ with his parents, as well as his fidelity to them. He had written from Newmarket on January 30, 1850, "I feel now as if I could do everything, and give up everything for Christ, and then I know it is nothing in comparison with his love. I ever remain your dutiful and affectionate son, Chas. H. Spurgeon."[37] In another letter, dated April 20, 1850, we see Spurgeon's desire to obey his parents. He requested permission to be baptized and demonstrated his willingness to obey their will. He anxiously wrote, "I have every morning looked for a letter from father, I long for an answer.... Do, if you please, send me either permission or refusal to be baptized; I have been kept in painful

---

36 "The Gospel in Power" in *The Metropolitan Tabernacle Pulpit*, 63:81.

37 C.H. Spurgeon, *The Letters of C.H. Spurgeon: Collected and Collated by His Son Charles Spurgeon* (Harrisburg: Good Books Corporation [1923]), 13.

suspense."[38] Spurgeon eagerly shared with his parents the success of his ministry. He wrote from Fairfield near Glasgow July 19, 1855, about his reception in Scotland, and he reaffirmed his love and devotion to his parents. He wrote, "Last Sabbath, I preached twice in Glasgow to immense crowds. I suppose mother is back, kiss her for me, and give my love to all. Best love to you my very dear father."[39] As an aside, it should be noted that on this occasion his modesty prevented him saying that over 20,000 were turned away![40] Other letters reveal his transparency with his parents regarding his own soul, as well as the ministry. In all of his extant letters, without exception Spurgeon conveys great warmth, love and affection. In all aspects he shows himself a devoted son.

2. Spirituality in marriage

Miss Susannah Thompson (1832–1903) was born on January 15, 1832. She was an irregular attendee of Park Street Chapel before she met Spurgeon. Her family was closely knit to Mr. and Mrs. Olney; Mr. Olney, a deacon, encouraged her to attend to hear the "boy preacher" from Waterbeach. Her earliest recollection of the boy preacher left her rather amused, and she recalls that the only thing she remembered from the sermon was "living stones in the Heavenly Temple perfectly joined together with the vermilion cement of Christ's blood."[41] However, as time went by, Susannah came under the conviction of sin when Spurgeon expounded Romans 10:8. She was further encouraged when Spurgeon gave her a copy of Bunyan's *Pilgrim's Progress*, dated April 20, 1854. Their friendship, although slow at first, soon began to blossom. At the opening of the Crystal Palace on June 10, 1854, Spurgeon handed a book to Susannah. It was Martin Tupper's *Proverbial Philosophy*. The young Spurgeon was pointing to the chapter on marriage! The opening verses ran, "Seek a good wife of thy God, for she is the best gift of His providence.... If thou art to have a wife of thy youth, she is now living on the earth; Therefore think of her, and pray for her

---

38 *The Letters of C.H. Spurgeon*, 20.
39 *The Letters of C.H. Spurgeon*, 44.
40 Hayden, *Highlights in the Life of Charles Haddon Spurgeon*, 8.
41 *The Early Years*, 281.

weal."[42] Susannah never forgot her future husband's words whispered in her ear, "Do you pray for him who is to be your husband?"[43]

The young couple were soon found strolling in the gardens of Crystal Palace where their hearts were united in love. Susannah reflects on that day and wrote, "From that time our friendship grew apace, and quickly ripened into deepest love—a love which lives in my heart to-day."[44] They were married on January 8, 1856, at New Park Street Chapel. A ten-day wedding trip to Paris followed in the spring and on September 20 of that year non-identical twins named Thomas and Charles were born to the happy Spurgeons.

Susannah would remain a steadfast helpmeet to Spurgeon. She wrote later: "I deemed it my joy and privilege to be ever at his side, accompanying him on many of his preaching journeys, nursing him in his occasional illnesses—his delighted companion during his holidays trips, always watching over and tending him with the enthusiasm and sympathy which my great love for him inspired."[45] Their love for one another never waned. Spurgeon's devotion is clearly seen in a beautiful love poem written to Susannah:

Married love—to my wife
C.H. Spurgeon

Over the space which parts us, my wife,
  I'll cast me a bridge of song;
Our hearts shall meet, O joy of my life,
  On its arch unseen but strong.

Beyond and above the wedlock tie,
  Our union to Christ we feel,
Uniting bonds wh[ich] were made on high,
  Shall hold us when earth shall reel.

---

42 *The Early Years*, 283.
43 *The Early Years*, 283.
44 *The Early Years*, 283.
45 *Autobiography*, 2:291-292.

> Though He who chose us all worlds before,
> Must reign in our hearts alone,
> We fondly believe that we shall adore,
> Together before His throne.[46]

Susannah was to become an invalid, yet she refused to make any demands upon her busy husband. The famous Sir James Simpson (1811–1870), a friend of the family, who discovered anaesthetic for operations and is named the father of modern gynaecology, operated on Susannah. A clue to her disabling illness is found in a book that was in Spurgeon's personal library, *A Practical Treatise on the Inflammation of the Uterus, the Cervix and on its Connections with other Uterine Diseases.*[47] The operation was without success. However, Susannah outlived her husband by ten years and died on October 22, 1903, at the age of seventy-one.

Although an invalid, Susannah encouraged Spurgeon in all his endeavours and also encouraged him to take needed rests to recoup in Menton, France, when his health demanded it. Her unselfish love and steadfast support of Spurgeon's ministry is clearly affirmed. We will summarize Susannah's devotion to her husband with this quotation cited by Charles Ray:

> I thank God, that he enabled me to carry out this determination [support the ministry] and rejoice that I have no cause to reproach myself with being a drag on the swift wheels of his consecrated life. I do not take any credit to myself for this; it was the Lord's will concerning me, and He saw to it that I received the necessary training whereby in after years I would cheerfully surrender His chosen servant to the incessant demands of his ministry, his literary work, and the multiplied labours of his exceptionally busy life.[48]

---

46 *Autobiography*, 2:298–299.

47 Thomas, "The Preacher's Progress" in Hulse, ed., *A Marvellous Ministry*, 39.

48 Cited in Charles Ray, *Mrs. C.H. Spurgeon* (1903; reprint, Indiana: Christian Book Gallery, 1994), 54–55.

Susannah Spurgeon
(1832–1903)

3. *Spirituality in the home*

We now look at Spurgeon's two sons. First let us hear a tribute from Thomas Spurgeon (1856–1917). Thomas Spurgeon succeeded his father to become pastor of the Metropolitan Tabernacle from 1893 to 1908. His esteem of his father's spirituality abounded:

> He to whose memory we pay our sad respect to-night, has been spoken of in his various capacities—preacher, author, tutor, benefactor; and right well the themes were handled; but there were only two men in the world fully qualified to speak of him as a father—and I, thank God, am one of these!
>
> The man who was so good to other people's children, was, you may be sure, a good father to his own. So busy a life prevented him from taking a very active part in the upbringing of his boys; besides, my precious mother was the best possible trainer. We learned from father's example rather than by his precept. And, if his home-life might be told, it would prove as striking as his public life. I fear me, we have not profited by it as we should; but it was bound to tell. There, at "home, sweet home," we marked his generosity, so unstinted that scarcely anyone appealed in vain, unless, indeed, he himself, just then, was as poor as the applicant, by reason of his constant giving. There we saw the daily, hourly, spirituality so natural and unconstrained, the trustful confidence in God, the humility which ever spake in praise of others, but never in his own.[49]

Let us now listen to Charles Spurgeon, Jr. (1856–1926) as he addressed his congregation at South Street Baptist Church, Greenwich. His admiration of his father's love, kindness and generosity overflowed:

> Never had any son kinder, wiser, happier, holier, or more generous sire; and I count it one of the highest honours of my life to place within the already well-stored casket, a few gems which

---

49 Thomas Spurgeon, advertising blurb, overleaf front cover, *The Metropolitan Tabernacle Pulpit*, vols. 62–63.

*A young Charles Spurgeon with his sons,
Thomas and Charles*

memory has preserved through that sweet relationship, which, in God's great goodness, I, as one of my father's sons was privileged to enjoy.

There was one trait in his noble and godly character which, among many others, always shone out with a lustre peculiarly its own. His humility was of a Christlike character, and it demands heartiest commendation from those who speak or write about him. Words of eulogy concerning himself were ever painful to him; his creed is this, as in all other matters, being "Not I, but Christ;" yet, from his own loving child some need of praise may surely come, and the son would fain render all due honour to the best of fathers. His blameless example, his holy consistency, his genial love, his generous liberality, his wise counsel, and his fearless fidelity to God and His truth, are all on a par with his fatherliness; and in my heart, as in all those with whom he came into contact, these qualities have been enshrined. The matchless grace and goodness, manifested in the home, found their counterpart in his public career, and proved how completely the spirit of the Master permeated the whole life of His servant. What my father was to me, to the Church of Christ, and to the world at large, none can ever fully estimate; but those who knew him best understood the secret of his magic power, for they felt that he "had been with Jesus," and that Jesus lived in him.[50]

Spurgeon's correspondence with his son Charles is inevitably characterized by warmth, love, concern and fatherly devotion. There is no question that genuine love abounded in the Spurgeon household.[51]

4. Comments on Spurgeon's spirituality by his friends

A few recollections of Charles Spurgeon by his friends will also testify to his spirituality. One such example is that of William Williams, pastor of Upton Chapel, London, a close and intimate confidant of Spurgeon. He wrote in his biography on Spurgeon:

---

50 *Autobiography*, 4:274.
51 *Autobiography*, 4:287–304.

"If you receive the heart of a friend," I once heard Mr. Spurgeon say, "mind you give him back your own." I count it one of the highest privileges of my life that I was one of many received into the big, brotherly heart of this mighty man of God.... All his talk was honesty personified; his life was as transparent as a sunbeam; his spirit guileless as that of "Israelite indeed." Grace seldom, if ever, produced a character which, for sterling integrity, for unsullied purity and noble generosity, excelled that of C.H. Spurgeon.[52]

In a letter written to Mrs. Spurgeon by the British prime minister, William Gladstone (1809–1898), he expressed concern over Spurgeon's failing health. Then Gladstone makes mention of Spurgeon's noteworthy character. He writes:

My Dear Madam, In my home, darkened at the present time, I have read with sad interest the daily accounts of Mr. Spurgeon's illness; and I cannot help conveying to you the earnest assurance of my sympathy with you and with him, and of my cordial admiration, not only of his splendid powers, but still more of his devoted and unfailing character.[53]

Spurgeon, although extremely weak, replied, "Yours is a word of love such as those only write who have been into the King's country, and have seen much of His face. My heart's love to you—C.H. Spurgeon."[54]

Anthony Ashley-Cooper (1801–1885), the seventh Earl of Shaftesbury, was another who greatly esteemed Spurgeon and corresponded regularly with him.[55] Shaftesbury not only enjoyed Spurgeon's gifts

---

52 William Williams, *Personal Reminiscences of Charles Haddon Spurgeon* (London: The Religious Tract Society, 1895), 12–13.

53 *Autobiography*, 4:358–359.

54 *Autobiography*, 4:359.

55 An important force in nineteenth-century British legislative reform, the Earl of Shaftesbury was instrumental in the passage of laws prohibiting the employment of women and children in coal mines (1842), reforming the care of the insane (1845) and establishing a ten-hour day for factory workers (1847). He also promoted the construction of model tenements for the poor, and model schools, called ragged schools,

but noted his character. Shaftsbury wrote:

> My Dear Friend,
> The books have arrived in safety; and to the inscription which you, yourself, have written,—I value it highly,—I shall add my own,—a prayer that my descendants will cherish the volumes as the gift of a man whom their ancestor honoured and loved as a private friend, but far more as a powerful, bold, true, single-hearted servant of our most blessed Lord and Saviour. God be with you and yours for ever and ever!
> SHAFTESBURY.[56]

Spurgeon loved and esteemed all who upheld the banner of the cross. His love overflowed beyond denominational boundaries. As an example, he greatly loved D.L. Moody who, although Arminian in theology, was kindred in spirit to Spurgeon. Moody preached at the Metropolitan Tabernacle and upon Spurgeon's death was given the pulpit Bible. Spurgeon also greatly admired Andrew Bonar (1810–1892), a Scottish Free Church minister whom Spurgeon once wrote asking for his autograph. He also esteemed the Anglican Bishop J.C. Ryle and immensely enjoyed his written works.

Spirituality in good works
The apostle James declared, "For as the body without the spirit is dead, so faith without works is dead also" (James 2:26, NKJV). This final section looks at how Spurgeon's pious works consumed him from morning to night as he laboured with the numerous tasks and responsibilities of his ministry.

A typical work week
The *Autobiography* provides insight into the various labours Spurgeon was engaged in throughout the week. On Sundays, Spurgeon would arrive early at the Metropolitan Tabernacle. Here he would deal with

---

for neglected poor children. The Shaftesbury Society merged with another organization in 2007 and is now known as Livability.

56 *Autobiography*, 4:179.

any urgent matters that may have arisen; select the hymns for the morning service and arrange with the precentor the best tunes. Interestingly, there were no musical instruments used in worship at the Metropolitan Tabernacle. The remaining time was spent in prayer with the elders and deacons who were available. At eleven o'clock, the morning worship service began as Spurgeon descended the steps to the platform, followed by a long train of office bearers. There, the great gospel-preacher poured out his soul to around 6,000! After the worship service, Spurgeon would meet with a long procession of friends and visitors, many of whom just wanted to shake his hand. On the second Sunday in the month, at the conclusion of the morning service, Spurgeon set aside time to meet with numerous Christian workers to encourage them as they undertook their various ministries in the afternoon: prayer, Sunday school, mission work and open-air preaching.[57]

After Sunday lunch and a brief rest, Spurgeon would retire at four o'clock to prepare for the evening service. Due to health problems, Spurgeon often stayed nearer the Tabernacle after the morning service. If so, much of the afternoon was absorbed in conversation with friends.

The evening service was usually shorter than the morning, with a greater emphasis on the gospel. Communion followed each evening service and would last about half-an-hour. At the communion table, Spurgeon gave some of his finest discourses.[58] At the conclusion of the service, Spurgeon was often found taking time to talk here and there with enquirers. The crowds were so overwhelming, that for a number of years, once every quarter, members of the church and congregation were asked not to come to the evening service but to give their seats to visitors. At the conclusion of this long day, if the week was peculiarly busy, Spurgeon would begin revising the morning sermon for publication.[59]

On Monday morning, Spurgeon would join his secretary Mr. J.W. Harrald and work through the mountain of letters that would pour in. Often, to encourage Spurgeon, Harrald would so arrange the corre-

---

57 *Autobiography*, 4:70–73.

58 For example see, C.H. Spurgeon, *Till He Come: Communion Meditations and Addresses* (Pasadena: Pilgrim Publications, 1978)

59 *Autobiography*, 4:74–75.

spondence that letters containing donations to the numerous ministries were on top. He also filtered out any hate mail that would pierce Spurgeon's sensitive heart. Spurgeon occasionally dictated replies, but more often wrote his own replies by hand. He believed that although arduous the task, it was an important ministry. The primary focus on Monday mornings was the revising of the Sunday's sermon for publication. The administration and correspondence generally continued to late afternoon.

At five-thirty p.m. Spurgeon would meet with the elders at the Metropolitan Tabernacle to discuss the spiritual welfare of the congregation or would attend a church meeting to welcome new church members. At times Spurgeon would be requested to attend the numerous annual meetings connected with the ministry of the church. His presence was always welcome especially at the annual meeting of the Poor Minister's Clothing Society, The Ladies' Maternal Society and the Ladies' Benevolent Society. Often he would leave the meeting early, placing it in the hands of his brother James Archer Spurgeon (1837–1899) or an elder, to start the prayer meeting. The prayer meeting began at seven and usually concluded at eight-thirty. Spurgeon conducted the prayer meeting, which he always considered the most important meeting in the week and the spiritual thermometer of the entire church. On some occasions, Spurgeon would leave early to fulfill preaching engagements elsewhere.[60]

Tuesday morning saw the final touches of the Sunday sermons for publication and further administrative duties. The afternoon was spent at the Tabernacle in pastoral duties. Here Spurgeon would meet between twenty and forty enquirers and candidates for baptism or church membership. This was a joy to Spurgeon who despite numerous and varied demands was a pastor at heart. At five o'clock Spurgeon would meet the leaders for tea and compare notes. Then, if necessary, he would return to the task until all were seen. Then he would go to the lecture hall and preside over numerous annual meetings: Sunday school, Almshouses Day Schools, Evangelistic Association, the Country Mission, The Loan Tract Society, The Spurgeon Sermons' Tract Society or Missions. So numerous were the annual

---

60 *Autobiography*, 4:79–82.

meetings that one could be scheduled every week! Spurgeon took particular joy in meeting new workers who often stood trembling before him! Often the Tabernacle would be open to other organizations from other denominations. Here he would be invited to give the annual address.[61]

Wednesday was Spurgeon's Sabbath-day. Here he tried to rest and was often found visiting close friends whose fellowship he prized. Noteworthy is his intimate friendship with Bishop Thorold (1825–1895), whom Spurgeon greatly loved and often visited on his day off.[62]

Thursday mornings were given over to correspondence and literary work in general. At times, Spurgeon felt overwhelmed:

> "I am only a poor clerk, driving the pen hour after hour; here is another whole morning gone, and nothing done but letters! letters! letters!" When reminded of the joy and comfort he was ministering to so many troubled hearts by that very drudgery, he agreed that it was for the Lord as truly as the preaching in which he so much more delighted.[63]

Spurgeon knew that his letters were an extension of his ministry and even when frivolous questions were asked, he refused to throw them away but, in kindness, answered them one by one. As time permitted, Spurgeon would spend the afternoons writing commentaries or other literary work. In the evening, from six to seven, Spurgeon was back at the Tabernacle attending what he termed, "The Pastor's prayer meeting." This extra gathering was for the sole purpose of pleading with God for his blessing upon the Word that was to be preached in the Sunday services. Spurgeon often left late after having to meet and converse with friends from various denominations.

On Friday morning, correspondence would often give way to preparing the president's address for his Friday afternoon lecturers from three to five p.m. at the Pastors' College. Here Spurgeon devoted all the powers of his mind and heart. These afternoon lectures became

---

61 *Autobiography*, 4:83–84.
62 *Autobiography*, 4:85–86.
63 *Autobiography*, 4:86.

the students' highlight of the week and helped to shape and prepare them for the gospel ministry.

> With such a responsive and appreciative audience, he was at his best; and both students and ministers have often declared that, not even in his most brilliant pulpit utterances, has he ever excelled, or even equalled, what it was their delight to hear from his lips in those never-to-be-forgotten days.[64]

After the lecture was over, Spurgeon met and conversed with the students, spending another hour ungrudgingly answering questions and dealing with any concerns. Periodically, Spurgeon would preach and have communion with the students.[65] After the Pastors' College lectures, Spurgeon, if not attending other meetings on the way home, would often visit church members.

Even when he was struck down through illness, Spurgeon steadfastly continued to preach. For example, he wrote:

> Westwood,
> April 5, 1881.
> Dear Friend,
> A month ago I was just recovering, and I took five services in the week with great delight. The immediate result was another illness. This time I am weaker, and I have the same work before me. The friends beg me not to attempt so much, and my own judgment tells me that they are right. I must therefore be away from the butchers' festival, though with great regret. I never promised to be there. Someone did for me, and I don't believe in those proxy promises. You are a host in yourself. Tell the true blues to be true blue, and follow the best of leaders,—namely, the Lord Jesus. May they all be pure and upright, so as to be Christians indeed. They will do well to be moderate in all things; better if they become total abstainers from strong drink; and best of all if they have new hearts and are believers in Jesus. I am sure we shall

---

64 *Autobiography*, 4:88.
65 *Autobiography*, 4:88–89.

always be glad to find house-room for them so long as you and the master-butchers find the solids for filling up the empties. I wish every man would get a day's march nearer Heaven on this occasion. May God's blessing be with you and all your hearers this night!

Yours heartily,

C.H. SPURGEON.

Conclusion

There is no doubt that Charles Spurgeon lived a life in the presence of God. His entire being was devoted to his Saviour with his life poured out on the altar of sacrificial service. Spurgeon was a man of God. His mind and heart portray a holy devotion; his character reflected Christlikeness, both in and out of public life. Despite his ministerial success he lived humbly, conscious that he was a debtor to grace alone. He lived in light of a heaven to gain and a hell to shun. His great joy was glorifying his God throughout his life and ministry and being used to gather in souls for God's kingdom. In every sphere, Spurgeon's spirituality represents a model to imitate and follow in the twenty-first century.

One of the last photographs taken of Spurgeon

10

Conclusion

This book clearly demonstrates that C.H. Spurgeon tenaciously upheld that ministerial success finds its antecedent in ministerial spirituality. In this regard, Spurgeon's life and thinking are models for the twenty-first-century pastor to emulate.

C.H. Spurgeon passionately pursued holiness in every aspect of his life and in every sphere of his ministry. From his *Autobiography* we have gleaned numerous instances of his love, faithfulness, kindness and generosity. In the *Metropolitan Tabernacle Pulpit* we have witnessed that his preaching was saturated with abounding love to Christ and the gospel; he also gave a valiant ongoing summons to his congregation to pursue holiness. His prayers, recorded in *C.H. Spurgeon's Prayers*, are potent as he pled for a sanctified people. His correspondence is overflowing with personal encouragements and earnest promotion of God's glory. His lectures at the Pastors' College set forth in *Lectures to My Students* and *An All-Round Ministry* overflowed with expectations and exhortations of ministerial spirituality exemplified in faithfulness and devotion to God. Susannah Spurgeon and her sons unquestionably testify to Spurgeon's love and gospel sincerity in that he practiced what he preached. Spurgeon was a giant among men, not because of his great oratory skill, neither his great intellect nor prolific writings, but because he was a man who passionately pursued and glorified a holy sovereign God. He took seriously his call to personal and ministerial holiness. Spurgeon was unashamedly convinced that ministerial spirituality is directly related to ministerial success—and hence, lack of spirituality to ministerial failure.

We have seen Spurgeon's passion to boldly and clearly articulate the unsearchable riches of the crucified Christ. Spurgeon unashamedly upheld the doctrines of grace and the sovereignty of God. His ministry was characterized by complete and utter dependence upon the enabling of the Holy Spirit, which continued throughout his glorious ministry. These words at the Metropolitan Tabernacle on March 31, 1861, would shape his ministry:

> If God shall bless us, He will make us a blessing to multitudes of others. Let God but send down the fire, and the biggest sinners in the neighbourhood will be converted; those who live in dens of infamy will be changed; the drunkard will forsake his cups, the swearer will repent of his blasphemy, the debauched will leave their lusts—
>
> Dry bones be raised, and clothed afresh,
> And hearts of stone be turned hearts of flesh.[1]

In addition, the convictions of a number of Baptist giants were examined and their impact upon the life and ministry of Spurgeon observed—John Bunyan, John Gill and Andrew Fuller—all of whom steadfastly advocated pastoral spirituality as an essential prerequisite for ministerial blessing. In this, Spurgeon was their heir.

His lectures at the Pastors' College, seen in *An All-Round Ministry* and *Lectures to My Students*, demonstrated Spurgeon's own thinking and personal conviction that ministerial spirituality is essential for a fruitful and successful ministry. This is particularly noteworthy in his last presidential address given to the Pastors' College: "The very root of holiness lies in the gospel of our Lord Jesus Christ."[2]

Finally, we considered Spurgeon's own spirituality as evident in his

---

1 "Temple Glories" in *The Metropolitan Tabernacle Pulpit*, vol. 7.
2 Spurgeon, *The Greatest Fight in the World*, 9.

hymn-writing, prayer life, personal relationships, letter-writing, sermons, worship, lifestyle and good works. Spurgeon saturated himself with the presence of God and the work of the gospel of Christ.

May it please almighty God, that we, like Spurgeon, might be diligent to polish our sabres with prayer, faithful to keep them sharp in truth, careful to remove every stain of sin, so that our ministries, like Spurgeon's, are characterized by an earnest pursuit of holiness, to experience the showers of blessing we long to see. May we be found faithful, as cavalry officers who one day will give their report to the Captain of the heavenly armies, to the glory of our God and King.

Editor's note

This book provides a practical workbook in the "Appendix" to encourage and promote personal spirituality for the busy twenty-first-century pastor and spiritual leader.

Appendix: A personal spiritual evaluation workbook

Based upon the model of C.H. Spurgeon's spirituality, these twenty-five questions are designed to envision and enrich present-day spiritual leaders in their pursuit of spirituality in life and ministry.

1. Spurgeon devoted himself to the lifelong passionate pursuit and enjoyment of God. List characteristics in your life that evidence your lifelong devotion to God.

_____
_____
_____
_____
_____
_____

2. How can this passionate pursuit of God be enriched in your life?

_____
_____
_____
_____

3. Spurgeon never lost his fervour of worship in every sphere of activity, despite numerous pressures and demands upon his time. List ways in which you cultivate a worshipful attitude throughout the day:

_____

_____

_____

_____

_____

_____

_____

4. Spurgeon saw prayer as a priority. How do you cultivate intimate fellowship with God through prayer? How can you develop this throughout your day?

_____

_____

_____

_____

_____

_____

_____

5. Spurgeon believed that a spiritual leader is so saturated with Scripture, that his very blood should be "Bibline." What systematic daily habits have you/will you cultivate in Scripture reading, meditation and memorization of God's holy Word?

_____

_____

_____

_____

_____

_____

6. Spurgeon saw Christian spirituality as a priority over gifts and capacity. How are you cultivating and developing Christian graces?

_____

_____

_____

_____

_____

_____

_____

_____

7. Spurgeon believed in a clear call to the gospel ministry. How does your call enrich and envision your ministry?

_____

_____

_____

_____

_____

_____

_____

_____

8. Spurgeon struggled with hardships, yet the call of God sustained him. How does God's call in your life and ministry uphold you in difficult times? List examples.

_____

_____

_____

_____

_____

_____

_____

_____

_____

_____

9. Spurgeon was God-centred throughout his ministry. He believed strongly in God's providential dealings and put his heart into the work. List evidences of God's providential dealings in your life and ministry:

_____

_____

_____

_____

_____

_____

_____

_____

10. Spurgeon, due to his heavy work load, got tired in the work but not of the work. Explain and illustrate in your own life what that means to you:

_____

_____

_____

_____

_____

_____

_____

_____

11. Spurgeon believed in Christocentric preaching and teaching. Is this characteristic of your style of preaching? How can you develop this further?

_____

_____

_____

_____

_____

_____

_____

_____

12. Spurgeon presented the gospel with great passion and plead with sinners to repent and come to Christ. Is this characteristic in your preaching? List examples:

_____

_____

_____

_____

_____

_____

_____

13. Spurgeon's pulpit prayers were urgent, passionate and bold. What characterizes your public prayers?

_____

_____

_____

_____

_____

_____

_____

14. Spurgeon enjoyed cultivating his own soul in the reading and meditation of the Puritan writers. Are your books sitting on the shelf or enriching your heart? Write out your personal reading plan. If it is not established, please do so now.

_____

_____

_____

_____

_____

_____

_____

_____

15. *Spurgeon's correspondence overflows with encouragement to fellow ministers and others. Do you encourage and promote spirituality in your correspondence? If so, how? If not, list six people who need encouragement and write to them.*

_____

_____

_____

_____

_____

_____

_____

_____

_____

16. *Spurgeon maintained an intimate relationship with Susannah, his wife. How is your relationship with your spouse? List 5 ways in which this can be enriched:*

_____

_____

_____

_____

_____

_____

_____

_____

17. *Spurgeon cultivated family worship in the home. How are you doing this on a daily basis?*

_____

_____

_____

_____

_____

_____

_____

18. Spurgeon enjoyed the love and respect of his children, Charles and Thomas. How are you cultivating love and respect from your children?

_____

_____

_____

_____

_____

_____

_____

_____

19. Spurgeon believed in visionary leadership. This is established in the Pastors' College, the construction of the Metropolitan Tabernacle and a host of Christian organizations. Articulate a five-year ministry vision plan below:

_____

_____

_____

_____

_____

_____

_____

_____

_____

_____

_____

_____

_____

_____

_____

_____

20. Spurgeon, as a result of the doctrines of grace, looked for evidences of Christ's blessing. What evidences have you seen that have encouraged you to stay in your sphere of ministry?

_____

_____

_____

_____

_____

_____

_____

_____

21. Spurgeon stood up for the truth, even at the cost of close friends. Are you willing to make a stand for the fundamentals of the faith? If so, how?

_____

_____

_____

_____

_____

_____

_____

_____

22. Spurgeon saw the training of ministers as his greatest task. How are you cultivating and training the leaders of tomorrow?

_____

_____

_____

_____

_____

_____

_____

23. *Spurgeon saw writing second to preaching as a means of shaping lives. How can you develop a writing ministry to promote spirituality among Christ's people?*

_____

_____

_____

_____

_____

_____

_____

_____

24. *Spurgeon was very conscious of the ministry of the Holy Spirit, not only in prayer meetings but also in his preaching. How can you develop a sensitivity and awareness to the promptings of God's Holy Spirit?*

_____

_____

_____

_____

_____

_____

25. *List things that you have learned from Spurgeon's life that will help you pursue spirituality:*

_____

_____

_____

_____

_____

_____

_____

Glossary

This glossary has relied heavily upon and quoted from *The Evangelical Dictionary of Theology* (Grand Rapids: Baker Book House, 1984), of which Walter A. Elwell was the editor.

Anglican: Anglicanism is a tradition within Christianity comprised of churches with historical connections to the Church of England, or similar beliefs, worship and church structures.

antinomianism: the doctrine that it is not necessary for Christians to preach and/or obey the moral law of the Old Testament.

Arminianism: the theological stance of Jacobus Arminius (1560–1609) and the movement which stemmed from his teachings. Its emphasis is on the free will of man and denial of God's sovereignty in salvation.

baptismal regeneration: a heretical doctrine which states that salvation is mediated through the act of baptism.

Baptist: a person who believes that the church is composed of those who have been regenerated by the Holy Spirit and brought to personal and saving faith in the Lord Jesus Christ. Baptism by immersion is for those who believe and have received Christ as Lord and Saviour [see the *First London Confession* (1644) and the *Second London Confession* (1689)].

Baptist Missionary Society: A Christian mission organization founded in England in 1792 with the purpose of outreach and evangelism.

believer's baptism: the doctrine which states that baptism is by immersion for those who believe in Christ as their Lord and Saviour. Baptism is a public declaration of the regenerating work of the Holy Spirit in the life and heart of the believer.

Calvinist: a person who holds to the teachings of John Calvin, whose work is summed up in what is best known as the doctrines of grace (see "the doctrines of grace").

Congregationalist: Congregationalism as a system appeared after the Reformation and Separatist movement in the late sixteenth and early seventeenth centuries.

Dissenter: a person in the sixteenth, seventeenth or eighteenth centuries who refused to belong to the Church of England.

evangelism: the proclamation of the good news of salvation in Jesus Christ with a view to bringing about the reconciliation of the sinner to God the Father, through the atoning work of Christ, by the regenerating power of the Holy Spirit.

exegetical: Exegesis is the drawing out of biblical truth from a text in its original, cultural context.

heterodoxy: that which is characterized by departure from accepted beliefs and standards; not orthodox, but not sufficiently different so as to be called heretical.

hyper-Calvinist: This view is above and beyond Calvinism. It emphasizes that because God predestines whom he wills to be saved, there is no need for evangelism and the free offer of the gospel.

infant baptism: the practice of baptizing babies and young children of believing parents. It is the belief that baptism is not primarily a sign of repentance and faith, but a covenant sign like circumcision.

Latitudinarian: one of a group of Anglican divines in the seventeenth century whose thought displayed a high regard for the authority of reason and a tolerant, antidogmatic temper. They reacted against the Calvinism of the Puritans and were broadly Arminian in outlook.

Liberalism: the movement away from traditional orthodoxy, in an attempt to harmonize biblical teachings with science, humanism or other secular fields. The denial of essential biblical doctrines such as the inerrancy of Scripture, the Trinity, the deity of Christ, his virgin birth, his resurrection and salvation by grace.

Modernism: See "Liberalism."

Nonconformist: Protestants who could not conscientiously conform to the Church of England, in particular after 1662. Nonconformists were comprised of Independents (Congregationalists), Presbyterians, Baptists and Quakers.

Oliver Twist: a story by Charles Dickens published in 1838 about an orphan named Oliver Twist, who is subjected to a miserable existence in a workhouse and then with an undertaker before he escapes to London, where he is led into the middle of a gang of pickpockets.

orthodox: Belief in the standards of accepted and true doctrines taught in the Bible.

Presbyterian: a person who is part of the system which emphasizes the importance of elders, or presbyters. Presbyterian churches identify with the *Belgic Confession* (1561), the *Heidelberg Catechism* (1563) or the *Westminster Confession* (1646).

Puritan: a member of a loosely organized reform movement originating during the English Reformation of the sixteenth century. The name came from efforts to "purify" the Church of England by those who felt that the Reformation had not yet been completed. Eventually the Puritans went on to attempt purification of the self and of society as well. The Puritans generally placed emphasis on four convictions: (1) that personal salvation was entirely from God, (2) that the Bible provided the indispensable guide to life, (3) that the church should reflect the express teaching of Scripture, and (4) that society was one unified whole. The Puritans believed that humankind was utterly dependent upon God for salvation.

Roundheads: supporters of Oliver Cromwell and Parliament during the English Civil Wars (1642–1646, 1648–1649 and 1649–1651).

Royalists: supporters of Charles I (1600–1649) during the English Civil Wars.

Sabellianism: The term "Sabellianism" comes from Sabellius, a theologian and priest from the third century. This heresy is also known as Modalism, which denies the Trinity. It declares that the Father, Son and Holy Spirit are different modes of the one God rather than three distinct Persons in the Godhead.

Salvation Army: William Booth founded the Salvation Army in 1865. It is a foundation which waged war on a dual front against poverty and the power of sin.

Socinianism: Socinus (1525–1562) was a heretic who denied original sin, predestination, the Trinity and the resurrection of the body. He also denied the deity and atoning work of Christ.

The Act of Uniformity: an act imposed in 1559 which reinforced the *Book of Common Prayer*. According to this act, every man must go to church once a week or be fined twelve pence.

the doctrines of grace: the foundational doctrines of Calvinism being comprised of five parts: (1) total depravity: the doctrine of man's complete inability to affect any righteousness—even faith—by his own power; every part and parcel of man is corrupted by sin; (2) unconditional election: the doctrine which states that before the foundation of the world God elected those whom he would save. Salvation is by God's grace, outside of time, and therefore not conditional upon our performance or station; (3) limited atonement: the doctrine which states that God has sovereignly elected some to salvation while passing over others by his sovereign will and for his glorious purposes; (4) irresistible grace: the doctrine which states that God's calling is effectual; that is, that God's election is a purposeful election which will result unequivocally in the salvation of the elect; (5) perseverance of the saints: the doctrine which states that God's elect will attain to glory. No trial or temptation will be so great that it removes us from Christ's hand. We are kept, secured and sealed by the blood of Christ and the indwelling of the Holy Spirit. This doctrine also states that Christ's people will prove themselves by their perseverance in faithfulness, truth and love.

The Down-Grade Controversy: a doctrinal controversy (1887–1889) in which Spurgeon was involved. The Down-Grade involved the undermining of the inspiration of Scripture, the deity of Christ, eternal punishment and other cardinal doctrines.

The Five Mile Act: an English law passed in 1665 that sought to enforce conformity to the established Church of England. Anyone who did not conform to the law were expelled. It forbade clergymen from living within five miles of a parish. Many ministers were deprived of their livelihoods under this act.

Victorian England: the United Kingdom during Queen Victoria's reign (1837–1901).

Select bibliography

Select works by Charles Haddon Spurgeon

Spurgeon, Charles Haddon, *An All Round Ministry*. Edinburgh: The Banner of Truth Trust, 1978.

——————. *Autobiography: The Early Years, 1834–1859*. Edinburgh: The Banner of Truth Trust, 1962.

——————. *Autobiography: The Full Harvest, 1860–1892*. Edinburgh: The Banner of Truth Trust, 1976.

——————. *C.H. Spurgeon's Autobiography: Compiled from His Diary, Letters and Records 1834–1892*. 4 vols. 1897-1900. Edited by Susannah Spurgeon and Joseph Harrald. Reprint, 4 vols. in 2, Pasadena, Texas: Pilgrim Publications, 1992.

——————. *C.H. Spurgeon's Prayers*. 1905. Reprint, Grand Rapids: Baker Book House, 1981.

——————. *Commenting and Commentaries*. London, 1876. Reprint, Edinburgh: The Banner of Truth Trust, 1969.

————. *Lectures to My Students*. 4 vols. 1875–1905. Reprint, Grand Rapids: Baker Books, 1980.

————. *Letters of Charles Haddon Spurgeon*. Edinburgh: The Banner of Truth Trust, 1992.

————. *Metropolitan Tabernacle Pulpit*. 63 vols. 1856–1904. Reprint, Pasadena: Pilgrim Publication, 1979.

————. *Our Own Hymn-Book: A Collection of Psalms and Hymns for Public, Social, and Private Worship*. Compiled by C.H. Spurgeon. 1866. Reprint, Pasadena: Pilgrim Publications, 2002.

————. *Pictures from Pilgrim's Progress*. London: Fleming H. Revell Company, 1903.

————. *The Down Grade Controversy: Collected Materials which Reveal the Viewpoint of the Late Charles Haddon Spurgeon … on one of the most significant disputes of his ministry*. Pasadena: Pilgrim Publications, 1978.

————. *The Greatest Fight in the World: C.H. Spurgeon's Final Manifesto*. 1891. Reprint, Albany: Ages Software, 1998.

————. *The Letters of C.H. Spurgeon: Collected and Collated by His Son Charles Spurgeon*. 1923. Reprint, Harrisburg: Good Books Corporation, n.d.

————. *The New Park Street Pulpit*. 6 vols. 1855–1860. Reprint, 6 vols. in 3, Pasadena: Pilgrim Publications, 1981.

————. *The Sword and the Trowel*. Edited by C.H. Spurgeon. 1865–1884. Reprint, Albany: AGES Software, 2000.

————. *Till He Come: Communion Meditations and Addresses*. Pasadena: Pilgrim Publications, 1978.

Spurgeon: secondary sources

Allen, James T. *Life Story of C.H. Spurgeon*. 1893. Reprint, Albany: Ages Software, 1996.

Bacon, Ernest W. *Spurgeon: Heir of the Puritans*. London: George Allen & Unwin, 1967.

Dallimore, Arnold. *Spurgeon*. Chicago: Moody Press, 1984.

Fullerton, W.Y. *Charles H. Spurgeon: London's Most Popular Preacher*. Chicago: Moody Press, 1966.

Greenwood, James. *The Seven Curses of London*. London, 1869.

Hayden, Eric. *Highlights in the Life of Charles Haddon Spurgeon*. Albany: AGES Software, 2000.

Hindson, Edward E. *Introduction to Puritan Theology*. Grand Rapids: Baker Book House, 1976.

Hulse, Erroll, ed. *A Marvellous Ministry: How the All-Round Ministry of C.H. Spurgeon Speaks to Us Today*. Darlington: Evangelical Press, 1993.

McCoy, Timothy Albert. "The Evangelistic Ministry of C.H. Spurgeon: Implications for a Contemporary Model for Pastoral Evangelism." Unpublished Ph.D. thesis. The Southern Baptist Theological Seminary, 1989.

Murray, Iain H. *Spurgeon v. Hyper-Calvinism: The Battle for Gospel Preaching*. Edinburgh: The Banner of Truth Trust, 1995.

Murray, Iain H. *The Forgotten Spurgeon*. Edinburgh: The Banner of Truth Trust, 1978.

Nettles, Thomas J. *By His Grace and For His Glory*. Grand Rapids: Baker Book House, 1986.

Page, Jesse. C.H. *Spurgeon His Life and Ministry*. London: Partridge and Co., 1892.

Pike, G. Holden. *The Life and Work of Charles Haddon Spurgeon*. 6 vols. 1894. Reprint, 6 vols. in 2, Edinburgh: The Banner of Truth Trust, 1991.

Ray, Charles. *Mrs. C.H. Spurgeon*. 1903. Reprint, Indiana: Christian Book Gallery, 1994.

John Bunyan

Brittain, Vera. *In the Steps of John Bunyan: An Excursion into Puritan England*. London: Rich and Cowan, 1950.

Buckland, A.R. *John Bunyan: The Man and His Work*. London: The Religious Tract Society, 1928.

Bunyan, John. *The Works of John Bunyan*. 3 vols. Edited by George Offor. Glasgow: Blackie and Son, 1860.

de Blois, Austen Kennedy. *John Bunyan the Man*. Philadelphia: Judson Press, 1928.

Loane, Marcus L. *Makers of Puritan History*. Grand Rapids: Eerdmans Publishing Company, 1961.

Piper, John. *The Hidden Smile of God: The Fruit of Affliction in the Lives of John Bunyan, William Cowper, and David Brainerd*. Wheaton, Illinois: Crossway Books, 2001.

Piper, John. "Suffering and the Sovereignty of God" in *The Southern Baptist Journal of Theology*, vol. 4, No. 2. 2000.

John Gill

Gill, John. *A Collection of Sermons and Tracts*. London: George Keith, 1773.

Gill, John. *Body of Divinity*. 1769. Reprint, Georgia: Turner Lassetter, 1957.

Fellows, John. *An Elegy on the Death of the Rev. John Gill, D.D.* London, 1771.

Haykin, Michael A.G., ed. *The Life and Thought of John Gill (1697–1771): A Tercentennial Appreciation*. New York: Brill, 1997.

Oliver, Robert. "John Gill," in Michael A.G. Haykin, ed., *The British Particular Baptists 1638–1910*. Springfield: Particular Baptist Press, 1998.

Andrew Fuller

Laws, Gilbert. *Andrew Fuller: Pastor, Theologian, Ropeholder*. London: Carey Press, 1942.

Fuller, Andrew. *The Complete Works of the Rev. Andrew Fuller*. 5 vols. Edited by Andrew Gunton Fuller. London: Holdsworth and Ball, 1831.

Phillips, David. *Memoir of the Life, Labors, and Extensive Usefulness of the Rev. Christmas Evans*. New York: M.W. Dodd, 1843.

Ryland, John. *The Work of Faith, the Labour of Love, and the Patience of Hope, Illustrated; in the Life and Death of the Reverend Andrew Fuller*. London: Button and Son, 1816.

Shindler, R. *From the Usher's Desk to the Tabernacle Pulpit: The Life and Labours of Pastor C.H. Spurgeon*. London: Passmore and Alabaster, 1892.

Wiersbe, Warren. *Walking with the Giants: A Minister's Guide to Good Reading and Great Preaching.* Grand Rapids: Baker Book House, 1976.

Williams, William. *Personal Reminiscences of Charles Haddon Spurgeon.* London: The Religious Tract Society, 1895.

Index

www.ingramcontent.com/pod-product-compliance
Lightning Source LLC
Chambersburg PA
CBHW021230090426
42740CB00006B/463